'*Buddhism for Pet Lovers* is a w[...] our animal companions. Pets gi[...] [...]y to practise the essence of six perfections of Buddhism—generosity, ethics, patience, perseverance, meditation and wisdom—for the benefit of beings that have taken non-human form in this lifetime. Our cherished pets are our Dharma friends and teachers.'

'In this riveting book, masterful storyteller David Michie explores Buddhist philosophy interweaving it with his deep love for animals and a profound understanding of holistic healing and energy work. You may have no knowledge of Buddhism, meditation, Reiki, holistic healing or hospice care. But if you have ever deeply loved an animal, this is, without doubt, the book for you.'

'A refreshing and insightful guide to finding ways to honour and cherish our animal friends each and every day. This gem of a book inspires us to find a deeper level of *being* to support the animals in our lives and in the world. Compassion and mindful presence in all stages of our animals' lives: there is no greater gift we can bring to the ones we love!'

'For animal lovers, pets are often our dearest and most sensitive friends and we love them with all our heart. David's book will help you to deeply strengthen your heart to heart bond with the pets in your life. At no time is this connection more important, than as the end of their precious life approaches.'

David Michie is an internationally published writer, meditation coach and Mindful Safari guide. He is author of the bestselling *Hurry Up and Meditate, Buddhism for Busy People, Why Mindfulness Is Better Than Chocolate*, and the popular Dalai Lama's Cat series of novels.

www.davidmichie.com

ALSO BY DAVID MICHIE

NON-FICTION

Buddhism For Busy People
Hurry Up and Meditate
Enlightenment To Go
Why Mindfulness Is Better Than Chocolate

FICTION

The Dalai Lama's Cat
The Dalai Lama's Cat and The Art of Purring
The Dalai Lama's Cat and The Power of Meow
The Queen's Corgi: On Purpose
The Magician of Lhasa

DAVID MICHIE

BUDDHISM
FOR
PET
LOVERS

SUPPORTING OUR CLOSEST
COMPANIONS THROUGH
LIFE AND DEATH

CONCH

CONCH BOOKS

First published in Australia in 2017

Copyright © Mosaic Reputation Management (Pty) Ltd 2017

CONCH

Conch Books, an imprint of Mosaic Reputation Management (Pty) Ltd.

Cataloguing-in-Publication details are available
from the National Library of Australia
www.trove.nla.gov.au

ISBN 9780994488145 (print USA version)
ISBN 9780994488152 (e-book USA version)

Set in 11/15 pt Adobe Garamond Pro by Bookhouse, Sydney
Cover design: Christabella Designs

Printed in the United States of America

Not to hurt our humble brethren (the animals) is our first duty to them, but to stop there is not enough. We have a higher mission—to be of service to them whenever they require it. If you have men who will exclude any of God's creatures from the shelter of compassion and pity, you will have men who will deal likewise with their fellow men.

SAINT FRANCIS OF ASSISI

A human being ... experiences himself, his thoughts and feelings as something separated from the rest—a kind of optical illusion of his consciousness. This delusion is a kind of prison for us, restricting us to our personal desires and to affection for a few persons nearest to us. Our task must be to free ourselves from this prison by widening our circle of understanding and compassion to embrace all living creatures and the whole of nature in its beauty.

ALBERT EINSTEIN

True happiness comes not from a limited concern for one's own wellbeing, or that of those one feels close to, but from developing love and compassion for all sentient beings.

THE DALAI LAMA

DEDICATION

THIS BOOK IS DEDICATED with heartfelt gratitude to my Dharma teachers: Geshe Acharya Thubten Loden, founder of the Tibetan Buddhist Society in Australia; Les Sheehy, director of the Tibetan Buddhist Society in Perth, Western Australia; and the Venerable Acharya Zasep Tulku Rinpoche, founder of Gaden for the West. I can never repay their kindness, and without them this book could never have been written.

This book is also dedicated to the many animals who have made my own journey through life immeasurably more fulfilling, fascinating and fun. Among my closest companions have been those possessing feathers or fur, our differences in no way lessening the deep bonds of affection we have shared. In writing this book, may I be creating the causes for them to quickly reach enlightenment. And may this book be a direct cause for more people to become interested in the consciousness of our fellow beings, and a motivation to us all to extend to all living creatures—especially those within our care—the time-honoured courtesy of treating others the way we ourselves wish to be treated.

May all beings have happiness
and the true cause of happiness;
May all beings be free from suffering
and the true cause of suffering;
May all beings never be parted
from the happiness that is without suffering;
May all beings abide in peace and equanimity,
their minds free from attachment, aversion and indifference.

CONTENTS

PARTNERS ON OUR JOURNEY THROUGH LIFE

HOW DO ANIMALS' MINDS compare to our own? Do pets have any purpose besides offering us companionship, cute social media photos and, perhaps, the motivation to exercise more regularly? And what happens to animals' consciousness when they die—does it continue in some way, and if so, how and where?

These are big questions for animal lovers because, for many of us, pets are among our most cherished family members. A constant presence in our homes, they are an important focus of our daily routine, active participants in our lives and silent witnesses to us in our most intimate and vulnerable moments. We share our valuable recreation time with them, our furniture, our belongings. Many of us even sleep in contorted postures so that they can share our beds!

We develop functioning, non-verbal communication with our animal companions covering not only domestic rules and rituals, but extending well beyond that to include a wide range of feelings, including playfulness, fear, anger and love. Over time, many of us bond very deeply with our pets, knowing that we share a mutual understanding and a profound connection on a level beyond words.

It's a connection with a quality we may not feel in relation to any other beings. What happens to our pets really matters.

For a growing number of people, it may matter even more than what happens to their fellow humans. One of the most pronounced demographic trends of the past quarter century has been the rise in single person households, which now comprise an astonishing 30 per cent of homes in the developed world. Missing from human-centric census figures are data for pets. If statistics were available, they may well reveal that, far from living alone, many of these 30 per cent-ers share their lives with dogs, cats, birds, rabbits, fish and other beings who are their de-facto families. Loved ones who must be cared for in old age, sickness and death by humans traversing the same ground, albeit more slowly, themselves.

In this, as in so many important ways, pets can be among our greatest gifts. Because in asking questions about what happens to our animal companions, we are propelled to seek answers about our own futures. In exploring practices that may benefit them, we, ourselves, become the first beneficiaries.

This book is about the inner lives of pets, written from the perspective of Tibetan Buddhism. And because of this unique and extraordinary vantage point, it is also about our own inner lives. For just as our pets are thinking, feeling beings with the capacity for transcendence, we are too.

Among my earliest memories is the face of Pandy, a Siamese cat my parents gave my older brother when I was born, to help assuage any feelings of jealousy he might feel towards the new arrival. Pandy was a much-loved companion throughout my childhood and right up till the time I graduated from university; she lived to the grand old age of twenty-one. As well as cats, my parents were keen on corgis, which is how two of these also became my energetic playmates during my school years. I was quite young when I discovered a strong empathy for animals. I can still remember being reduced to tears in the back of the family car when a weekend excursion took us past a herd of cattle trapped in barren fields behind a barbed wire fence, so malnourished that their ribs and spines were clearly visible through their hides: how was it possible people could be so unfeeling that they would allow such a thing to happen, I wondered?

As a child I was devoted to a white rabbit, a golden hamster, a guinea pig and several mice—though seldom concurrently. A cockatiel was perched on my shoulder through most of my teenage years, by which time Pandy's hunting instincts had, fortunately, dimmed. Because I grew up in Zimbabwe, school holidays frequently meant a visit to a game reserve, and during one vacation I volunteered at the Lion and Cheetah Park, where my duties ran to bottle-feeding lion cubs and the showering of an orphaned baby elephant.

Doctor Dolittle wasn't so much my childhood hero as my role model! Why would anybody *not* wish to talk to the animals, parlay with the pachyderms or chat to a chimp in chimpanzee? I devoured every book written by Gerald Durrell and James Herriot, and fully intended to become a vet until the age of sixteen, when a short stint observing what went on behind the scenes at our local veterinary clinic made me realise that the clinical requirements of being a vet demanded very different skills from those I possessed. It was only much later that I worked out a way to use my compulsion for writing to be of benefit to those possessing fur, feathers and fins.

Throughout my rich and diverse encounters with different crea-tures, it never occurred to me that any of them was fundamentally different from me. On a daily basis we all sought food, drink and whatever creature comforts were on offer. Just as we did our best to avoid hardships of any kind. We all enjoyed giving and receiving affection. And we also had our quirks and rebellious streaks; in the case of Toto, the cockatiel, at the end of the afternoon he would sometimes remain stubbornly in the highest branches of the cherry tree, so that after all coaxing failed, only a well-aimed tennis ball—softly thrown, of course—would persuade him to fly back down again.

UNANSWERED QUESTIONS

The deaths of my pets were not only the cause of grief, but also of unanswered questions. My parents were church-going Presbyterians, and when I asked our kindly minister about the fate of poor Bugs, the first to die, he gave me an answer that was intended to reassure but didn't. What I wanted to be told was that Bugs was hopping happily in heaven, cared for by rabbit-loving angels and enjoying shredded lettuce from the bottom tray of celestial tea trolleys—an indulgence she'd been allowed at home. Our reverend's assertion that we could trust God to take care of all His creatures had a vagueness about it that perplexed me.

It was a perplexity that continued as I grew older and discovered that across Christian traditions there is no consensus about the inner lives of animals. What I found instead was ambiguity and contradiction about even the most basic of facts, such as whether or not animals have souls—a bewildering paradox given that the word 'animal' comes from the Latin *animalis*, meaning having soul, or having breath. Revolting, as a teenager, I used to question why, among the seemingly endless Old Testament litanies of who begat whom, the Good Lord hadn't thought it useful to devote a chapter or two to outlining the spiritual prospects of the overwhelming majority of our world's inhabitants.

If not religion, then what about science? What had the greatest thinkers in the Western world to say about this important subject? As it turned out, not very much. For most of its history, the focus of Western science has been on the external, measurable world, with inquiry extending to consciousness only recently. And during the past 200 years, the dominant ideology of science has been materialism— that is, the view that matter is the only thing that exists. In the words of Francis Crick, co-discoverer of DNA and Nobel Prize Laureate: 'You, your joys and your sorrows, your memories and your ambitions, your sense of personal identity and free will, are in fact no more than the behaviour of a vast assembly of nerve cells and their associated molecules . . .'[1]

Not all scientists would agree with these words. Those involved in the field of quantum physics would question whether the workings of the mind can be explained on the basis of classical mechanics. If matter is also energy, then any explanation that ignores the non-material properties of the body cannot possibly tell the whole story.

In recent years, part of the groundswell towards greener, healthier and more mindful living has been the explosion of research studies, TV programs and books focusing on animals and our relationships with them. Veterinarians, biologists and conservationists have been joined by new breeds of animal experts, including behaviourists, communicators and complementary healers. Through their work we have come to learn that the other species with whom we share our planet possess many of the qualities believed, until recently, to be uniquely human, and that some possess powers that we'd consider to be superhuman if they were exercised by people. Pigs have IQ levels similar to chimpanzees, live in complex social communities and display high levels of self-awareness and empathy when witnessing the same emotion in other pigs.[2] Elephants grieve and mourn the death of their family members and demonstrate very high levels of mutual support.[3] Dolphins and other cetaceans can see in 3D. Dogs can be trained to detect dangerous falls in a diabetic's blood sugar level, can know in advance if someone is about to have an epileptic seizure and can even detect bladder cancer with astounding reliability.[4] Some cats, parrots, horses and dogs have shown that they can accurately predict when their human companions are on their way home, as well as exhibit other startling examples of telepathy.[5]

Increasingly, we are coming to realise that just because animals don't communicate like we do, it doesn't mean they are less sentient. They are thinking, feeling beings with the same capacity as ourselves for empathy and selfishness, rage and compassion, fear and altruism. In terms of sensory capacity, many of them possess capabilities well beyond our own.

WE ARE ALL SENTIENT BEINGS

In my early thirties I began meditating to help manage stress. I was living in London, working for a public relations agency, an environment that was stimulating but relentless. Within weeks of taking up meditation practice I began to experience its benefits in ways which went beyond stress management. Eager to know more about the theory behind the simple, morning ritual, I found myself increasingly drawn to books about Buddhism, having discovered that meditation lay at the heart of this tradition.

One thing led to another and I started attending Buddhist classes. This was when, while no longer looking, I found answers to the questions that I had long since given up on. Here, at last, was an approach to both animal and human consciousness that was straightforward and accorded with my own experience. For the thousands of years that Western scientists had been trying to make sense of external reality, their Eastern peers had been doing the same thing in relation to inner reality, using the very same methods of long-term, forensic observation, rigorous testing of hypotheses, peer review and debate. The end result was a coherent explanation that not only made sense as a theory but could also be used as a practical basis for our own explorations of the mind.

Yes, of course animals have consciousness, is the Buddhist view. And yes, one mind moment is affected by previous mind moments in a causal way so that, whether we are aware of it or not, on an ongoing basis, we are shaping the way we experience reality. Yes, too, the mind, which may be defined as a continuum of clarity and cognition, is non-material, or energetic in nature, and continues beyond physical death in a subtle form.

Newcomers to Tibetan Buddhism frequently remark on how many of the teachings seem to them to be common sense, which makes for a reassuring foundation. But the teachings go well beyond an acknowledgement of the obvious. Of special interest to animal lovers is the concept of bodhichitta (pron. bode-ee-cheetah) which, more than any other term, distinguishes the Tibetan Buddhist tradition. Derived from two Sanskrit words, *bodhi*, meaning awake or enlightened, and *citta,* meaning mind or heart, bodhichitta is the mind of enlightenment, and may be defined as the wish to attain enlightenment to be of ultimate benefit to *all* sentient beings. Based on compassion for the suffering we can see for ourselves among both humans and animals, the central objective of Buddhist practice is to cultivate our bodhichitta motivation until it becomes spontaneous and heartfelt.

There is nothing human-centric about bodhichitta. It is explicitly all-inclusive. Even a goal as sweeping as helping every person on the planet attain a state of enlightenment would be flawed: it would fail to recognise that all living beings share the same essential nature. We are all sentient beings.

PARTNERS ON OUR JOURNEY THROUGH LIFE

The title of this book refers specifically to pets. You may be wondering why I am not writing about Buddhism in relation to *all* animals?

The guiding principles I outline in Chapter Three can be applied equally to your beloved animal companion as to a herd of giraffes you may watch moving gracefully into the sunset while on safari. What makes pets different is our connection to them. Of the countless billions of sentient beings on planet earth, the fact that we share our homes with a specific few is, from a Buddhist perspective, no accident. The principal of cause and effect, or karma, suggests that the beings closest to us in this life are those with whom we have a particularly strong connection.

Whatever our belief system, the interactions we have with our pets on an ongoing basis offer far greater scope for mutual engagement than the relatively few moments we may spend in the presence of, say, mountain gorillas in the mists of Central Africa, however precious those moments may be. Our pets are part of our world 24/7. Sometimes we spend more time with them than even our closest friends.

On the surface of things, it may seem that people provide food, shelter and walking services in exchange for affection, and perhaps, in the case of dogs, an element of security. But we don't have to delve too deep to recognise that our relationship with pets is a lot more complex than this basic trade-off would suggest. What if, as psychologists tell us, our emotional wellbeing depends on our mindfulness, openness, generosity, resilience and spontaneity? Do pets not offer us ample opportunity to cultivate these each and every day? Are they not, according to this view, among our most active supporters in providing countless opportunities to enhance our capacity for contentment?

The transformative presence of pets is now widely recognised in retirement homes, where lounges filled with sedentary, disengaged residents come alive with the appearance of a visiting golden retriever or a therapy cat. The simple presence of a pet can offer a lightness and a joy, a sense of connection, and an invitation to be uninhibitedly ourselves in a way that is both unique and priceless.

And from a Buddhist perspective, for those of us who wish to help others find not only mundane contentment but also to realise their ultimate potential, the pets in our lives represent a precious and awesome privilege. As I outline on the following pages, there are a great many practices that provide powerful imprints on our pets' consciousness. These range from ongoing activities like being mindfully present for them every day, and creating positive associations with powerful mantras, to the extraordinary opportunity presented by a pet's death, when we have the chance to help them navigate through a time of transition for the best possible outcome.

I refer to dogs and cats a lot in this book, reflecting their popularity as pets, and the depth of our experience living closely with them. It's important to know that exactly the same principles and practices apply to other animals. Mice, hamsters, rats and other rodents are very much a part of our broader, mammalian family. It is striking that the reason why rats are the animal of choice for laboratory testing is precisely because their physiological functioning is so similar to our own. Pigs' heart valves are routinely transplanted into humans. We are all of the same ilk.

Rabbits and guinea pigs can be affectionate pets. Pot-bellied pigs are adored by their owners. And the very close relationship some people enjoy with horses shows that what matters here is not shape or size but consciousness.

The complexity of birds' brains is only now beginning to be understood—the old insult could not be more misleading. Our avian friends are certainly as sentient as we are. And while warm bonds of friendship are less frequently reported with fish and reptiles, the mere fact that they possess minds means that we can help them, if perhaps to a lesser extent than those beings with whom we have a more empathetic connection.

Do you need to believe there is some continuation of life after death to find the practices in this book useful? Must you accept karma—the principle that all actions create effects in the minds of those undertaking them, whether human or animal? Do you have to buy into the concept of rebirth or other aspects of Eastern mysticism that you may find, frankly, weird?

No. You don't have to believe anything. What you *do* need is an open mind.

The materialist theory that consciousness arises from the brain can no more be proven than the idea that consciousness is shaped by cause and effect can be disproven. If you are new to some of these concepts, they may take time to get your head around.

One of the most exciting aspects of Tibetan Buddhism is that it is a living tradition. Residing among us, here today, are lamas and spiritual masters such as my own precious teachers, Geshe Acharya Thubten Loden, Venerable Acharya Zasep Tulku Rinpoche and Les Sheehy, who walk the talk. The more you spend time with them, and observe their actions, the more self-evident the truth of their teachings becomes. They are, if you like, the living, breathing embodiment of this wisdom tradition. Texts and ancient scriptures are all very well, but what validates them and makes them real for Buddhists is the way we can see them transform the lives of others—as well as our own.

For many of us, pets are among the handful of beings who are our closest companions on our journey through life. We may already greatly value these relationships. What I hope to describe, in the pages that follow, is how they can become of inconceivably greater value. How we can work with the love and joy we already feel in these very special relationships to energise and enrich both our pets' development as well as our own. How what starts out as the simple wish for the happiness of our beloved pet, when conjoined with bodhichitta, becomes the transcendental cause not only for our pets' ultimate enlightenment, but for ours too.

What happened to Bugs? My biggest regret is that I didn't know then what I know now, or I could have been of far greater help to her. What I am confident of is that her mind stream continues. Through our close connection there is the prospect that I can be of benefit, and the sooner I evolve in my own journey, the faster I will be of use to her.

Ultimately, we may one day be able to manifest as two beings at a celestial tea trolley, joking about the time that one of us was a rabbit and the other a human being—and perhaps contrast it with the time when it was the other way around.

Or maybe she is with me as I write these words, at this very minute, lying on the end of my desk, now in the guise of my tortoiseshell cat, purring . . .

CHAPTER ONE

HOW DOGS AND CATS CAME INTO OUR LIVES

Abby, a four-month-old West Highland terrier, helped her Mum's heart heal after she lost her previous pooch to cancer. Abby is a sweet puppy whose favourite things in the world are shoes—to chew! ALEX CEARNS/HOUNDSTOOTH STUDIO

THE PRESENCE OF PETS in our lives is something we often take for granted. But for most of the 200,000 years that humans have lived on earth, our lives have not been enmeshed with those of other species in the way they are today.

To understand where we find ourselves now, it's helpful to take a brief look at where we have come from. How we and our closest companions—in particular our most popular pets, dogs and cats—first came into contact. The challenges our relationships have faced along the way. And how we have recently begun to witness the convergence of cognitive scientists, neurobiologists, ethologists, behaviourists and others in exploring the intriguing and multi-dimensional world of animal consciousness.

MAN'S FIRST FRIEND

Dogs came into our lives around 15,000 years ago. In those days, we were Stone Age cave dwellers and they were wolves. *Canis lupus* is the Latin name for a wolf and today's dog, *Canis lupus familiaris*, is genetically almost identical. I sometimes marvel at the fact that little Trixabelle, the pampered chihuahua in the diamante collar is, to all intents and purposes, a miniature wolf.

The *familiaris* at the end of the Latin name gives the key to how Trixabelle, rather than some other wolf, came to find herself ferried round town in a Prada handbag. Sometime in the distant past, the wolves hanging around Stone Age settlements to pick at charred remains became friendly with the Flintstones. More *familiaris*. Perhaps it was the world's first rescue pups who began the integration of wolves with human society. Hard though it may be for us to imagine today, until very recently wolves were extremely common. In the United States and Mexico alone, before the arrival of Europeans, an estimated one million wolves roamed the continent. By 1930, they had been wiped off 95 per cent of their land.[1]

If wolves initiated the domestication process, becoming man's first friend, they were well served by some important canine abilities. Dogs are natural alarm systems and guards, alerting their human family to the approach of other people and potential predators. They are playmates for children, living vacuum cleaners for caves and huts, sources of warmth on cold winter nights, trackers and guides for food and natural hunting partners.

In the wild, wolves need to be tuned into where the attention of their fellow pack members is focused. In the same way, dogs know exactly where a person's attention is placed. Throw a stick for a dog, before setting off in a different direction, and the dog will return with the stick to wherever you are facing. Without training, a dog will understand what you mean when you point somewhere—a non-verbal cue that even some primates don't follow.

EXPERT BODY LANGUAGE READERS

Recent work by Charlotte Duranton of Marseille University confirms how dogs are expert at reading the body language, or non-verbal communication, of their owners. In an article that appeared in *Animal Behaviour* journal, Duranton explained how dogs study the signals given by their owners when deciding whether a stranger is a friend or foe. When owners retreat from a stranger, the dogs look at the stranger significantly sooner and take much more time to approach them than if their owner walks towards the stranger. Dogs also interact more with their owners when they retreat than when they don't.[2]

A different study by psychologists Deborah Custance and Jennifer Mayer of Goldsmiths College in London also proved that dogs not only empathise but also sympathise with people when they are distressed. Modifying a procedure used to measure empathy in human infants, they tested eighteen dogs in their owners' homes. In each case the dog's owner and a stranger sat a short distance apart and engaged in a sequence of activities—speaking, pretending to cry or humming in an unusual way—while being filmed.

The crying was, of course, the behaviour that would reveal empathy. If the dog was upset by crying, approaching its owner may be interpreted as merely seeking comfort for itself. But if the stranger cried, given that the dog has no bond with the stranger, it would have no reason to nuzzle the stranger's hand, put its head on the stranger's lap, or offer some other comforting behaviour.

The researchers found that, like human toddlers, dogs would approach the strangers as well as their owners when they appeared to be upset, even though they had no previous bond. In other words, dogs not only feel empathy, but also show sympathy.[3]

While these findings may seem like a statement of the obvious to dog lovers, it is significant that scientists are studying canine cognition at all. Only a generation ago the consensus view would have been that canine cognition was an impossibility for the simple reason that dogs were believed to be incapable of thought, let alone complex affective states like empathy.

One of the positive aspects of the digital age is the way in which stories can quickly be shared. I was intrigued by a dazzling display of canine cognition in a story quoted in the media, about how a New Jersey dog saved the life of its critically ill owner by smashing a window to alert passers-by. Trapped inside the house with its owner, who had been incapacitated for some time, when the dog heard two women talking as they walked past the home, he broke the glass of a window with his paws to get their attention. The women approached the house and the clearly agitated dog. When they could get no answer from inside, they called for an ambulance, and within a short while, the dog's owner was taken to intensive care, thereby saving his life.[4]

A separate story tells of how a couple in Livonia, New York, rescued a golden retriever from a park where they had found him, starving to death. A year later, the woman woke up to find Teddy the retriever in their bedroom, although normally he slept downstairs. Moments later, the woman smelled smoke. Shaking her fiancé awake, the two of them, plus their two boys and Teddy the dog, hurried from the house. Ten minutes later, the home in which they had been sound asleep had turned into a fireball.[5]

Step by step we are coming to a belated understanding of the many ways in which dogs are keenly attuned to their owners and demonstrate clear evidence of intelligence, understanding and the ability to act with speed and compassion. The capacity to read facial expression and other non-verbal communication is a part of the way they understand us. Beyond this, however, is another ability that most dog lovers have experienced at one time or another: dogs seem able to tune into our thoughts in a telepathic way.

CANINE TELEPATHY

How frequently is it that you look outside, take in the good weather and decide that it would be great to go for a walk when, turning round, you find your pet pooch has materialised beside you from the other end of the house? Perhaps even carrying his leash? Or maybe you have experienced the opposite: knowing that it's about time to head off to this morning's inoculation appointment at the vet, you search for your dog, only to discover that he has somehow vanished?

These are fairly typical examples of canine telepathy, a concept that has defied objective validation until recently. Biologist Rupert Sheldrake has long been willing to go where other scientists feared to tread in seeking to establish evidence of animal telepathy. Sheldrake studied natural sciences at Cambridge University where he took a PhD in biochemistry; was a Fellow of Clare College, Cambridge, where he was Director of Studies in cell biology; and is currently a Fellow of the Institute of Noetic Sciences in California. He has helped design controlled trials investigating phenomena such as the one that some dogs seem able to know when their owners are coming home, a trial replicated by researchers elsewhere. Having had reports from a variety of families that their dogs would get up from wherever they were resting and move towards the front door or porch in anticipation of their owner's return from work, Sheldrake set out to test whether this really was telepathy, or simply habit.

Participating owners in the experiment were told to leave their workplaces at random times, and return home using a variety of transport methods, while video cameras set up in their homes made a record of a dog's behaviour. Time and again it was established that the dogs really were picking up on what was happening with their owners. A pattern emerged that, irrespective of the time the owner left work, or how long the journey home would be, it was always the owner's *intention* to return home that triggered dogs' behaviour to get up and wait for the front door to open.[6]

Other studies have been undertaken by new generations of scientists attempting to understand the nature of intuition and telepathic communication with animals. The relationships we have with our pets can rarely be defined in terms of the purely mechanistic. Just as with our most precious human relationships, the glue that holds us strongest arises from the emotional bonds we share, the understanding, empathy and wish for one another's happiness which goes beyond words or concepts and connects us at a deeper level.

I recently heard a story from regional Western Australia about a dog who, as a playmate and friend, was devoted to a young man, who subsequently enlisted to fight in the Second World War. After training, the soldier was sent to Europe and an unknown future. One night, for no apparent reason at all, the dog leapt up from where it was lying with the rest of the family, and began howling in the most distressed way before running into the night. It was never seen again.

The rest of the family were terribly shaken—not only by what had happened, but because of what they intuitively knew it signified.

Two days later, they received a telegram confirming that their son and brother had indeed been killed in action.

THEN CAME CATS

It's not until 10,000 years ago that we find evidence of cats' place in human society. Humans had to evolve from hunter gatherers into farmers before a useful role could be found for Miss Puss, who soon found herself appointed to the role of Chief Pest Controller.

The first human farmers, storing their harvests in granaries, would have soon discovered that their harvest attracted the unwanted attention of rodents who, in turn, attracted the interest of wild cats. Our Neolithic forebears would have observed cats' superlative skills in tracking, patiently awaiting and silently dispatching rats and mice. They would have identified a natural ally. One for whom it was certainly worth sacrificing a few scraps of meat if it meant keeping them around to help protect next year's harvest.

For thousands of years cats continued to live on the periphery of human society, tolerated so long as they served a useful purpose. As with dogs, it is likely that domestication began haphazardly and in different places when cats went beyond being mere service providers to engage people's affections as well.

The first firm evidence that cats had become domesticated is found in Egyptian art from between three and four thousand years ago, almost always in the homes of noble families. Egyptian aristocrats were very fond of cats. One royal scion, Crown Prince Thutmose, the son of Pharaoh Amenhotep III, was so devoted to his cat Osiris, Ta-Miaut (Osiris the She Cat) that when she died he had her embalmed and placed in a sarcophagus engraved with the poetic affirmation: 'I bristle before the Sky, and its parts that are upon it. I myself am placed among the imperishable ones that are in the Sky. For I am Ta-Miaut, the Triumphant.'

SACRED ANIMALS

The quality of cats to inspire the metaphysical imagination of humans has been both a blessing to their species as well as a terrible curse. Bastet, a cat-headed goddess, was worshipped by the Egyptians as early as 2890 BC. She was associated with fertility, female sexuality and being a good mother—qualities of most domestic cats. In time, Bastet found her way into Greek mythology as Artemis, their own moon goddess; in Roman mythology, known as Diana, the goddess of the hunt, wild animals, childbirth and virginity. As creatures of the night it seems entirely appropriate that cats should have been so closely associated with the moon and lunar symbolism since the earliest of times.

Herodotus, the fifth century Greek historian, leaves us in no doubt about the veneration with which Egyptians held their cats. If a pet cat died, it was commonplace for every family member to shave their eyebrows out of respect. What's more, the annual festival of Bubastis, in honour of Bastet, was the most joyful and elaborate on the Egyptian calendar, and 'more wine of the grape was drank in those days than in all the rest of the year. Such was the manner of this festival: and, it is said, that as many as 700,000 pilgrims have been known to celebrate the Feast of Bast at the same time.'7 Quite some party, even by today's standards!

While the worship of cats continued in Egypt, the goddess Bastet was probably a high water mark for them, because this reverence for cats morphed into a different and hideous expression. Cats became 'sacred animals' to be bred, killed, mummified and offered to the gods.

The production of sacred animals was big business in ancient Egypt, and archaeologists have discovered the remains of large catteries in the vicinity of temples, along with vast heaps of cat bones. This extreme devotion to a feline goddess, combined with a willingness to sacrifice mummified cats, was a disturbing dichotomy in attitudes which continued to rumble through history.

CATS AS FAMILIARS

In Europe, right through the Middle Ages, cats were valued as pest controllers and adored by many as pets, but there was the constant undertow of their associations with the occult. Being a perennial favourite pet of older women, in an era of illiteracy and ignorance, all too often cats were cast in the role of 'familiars', spirits who had taken animal form to help a witch perform magic. The sorcery being carried out was not always believed to be malevolent, but given the pagan roots of the worship of the mother goddess, it was most certainly not Christian.

Perhaps some of the older women may have intuitively understood, as many seniors do today, the mysterious but scientifically validated qualities of cats to enhance our physical wellbeing. The rate at which cats purr has been shown to heal bones and muscles—part of the reason that they do it. Just listening to a cat purring is wonderfully de-stressing. These qualities may be part of the reason why cat owners are 30 to 40 per cent less likely to die of cardiovascular disease than people who don't have cats in their homes, according to a longitudinal study conducted by the University of Minnesota Stroke Institute.[8] An extraordinary statistic.

Today it may be easy to be dismissive of cat hatred in the Middle Ages, but it became so widespread and strongly held that, in 1233, Pope Gregory IX issued a papal bull, identifying cats in general, and black cats in particular, with Satan and campaigning for their extermination. According to cat expert John Bradshaw, 'Over the next 300 years, millions of cats were tortured and killed, along with hundreds of thousands of their mainly female owners, who were suspected of witchcraft. Urban populations of cats were decimated.'[9]

Americans had their share of exactly the same prejudices in the form of the Salem Witch Trials of 1692–93, which also heard accounts of evil and vexatious spirits transmuting themselves into the form of a variety of cats.

It wasn't until after The Enlightenment that cats were able to shake off their Satanic associations and take their place, alongside dogs, in the homes of Europe's royal families, the aspirational models of the time.

CATS AND NON-VERBAL COMMUNICATION

Cats have been just as successful as dogs in becoming part of the fabric of our lives. Like dogs, they have had to adapt to us, rather than the other way around, and although with some cats, you have the distinct impression that they are doing so only with the greatest reluctance, this impression has a lot more to do with our own projection than anything else!

Cats, unlike dogs, are not social creatures. In the wild, male cats live alone, and female cats, together with young, male offspring, form only small groups. Their survival is based not on collaboration, but on competition. Concealing one's thoughts and feelings is therefore part of a cat's evolutionary inheritance. But, as every cat lover knows, even though cats are more enigmatic about what they observe, think and feel, it would be a mistake to underestimate what is going on beneath their apparently aloof exterior.

Research conducted by Isabella Merola and colleagues at the University of Milan set out to establish if cats seek emotional information provided by their owners about new or unfamiliar objects to guide their own behaviour—much like the study described earlier in this chapter for dogs. Four out of five cats looked to their owners for an emotional cue when presented with an unfamiliar object—a similar proportion as in dogs. For much of the time our cats may wear a poker face, but we can be certain they are observing our reactions very closely and responding to them.[10]

A study conducted by animal behaviourist John Bradshaw shows just how closely. Bradshaw set out to find if there was any truth to the legend that cats are magnetically drawn to people who dislike or are allergic to them, and will immediately try to jump on their lap. After he recruited a number of cat-phobics, as well as cat lovers—all male, because Bradshaw couldn't find any cat-hating women—subjects were told they had to sit on a couch and not move, even if a cat tried to sit on their lap. A number of different cats took part in the experiment. According to Bradshaw:

> The cats, for their part, seemed to sense the disposition of the people they were meeting within a few seconds of entering the room. They rarely approached the cat-phobics, preferring to sit near the door and look away from them. It was unclear how the cats were detecting the difference between the two types of men: perhaps they could sense that the cat-phobics

were tenser, or smelled different, or glanced nervously at the cats. Nevertheless, the cats' reactions show that they can be keenly perceptive when encountering someone for the first time.

There was one cat, however, who would single out the cat-phobics for attention, jumping on their laps and purring loudly. Evidence of a perverse streak?! Bradshaw suggests that cats, such as this one, make a lasting impression on cat-phobics, which is why the myth of the cat hater attracting unwanted feline attention continues.[11]

PSYCHIC CATS

Cats may be expert body-readers, but what about their ability to tune into their owners? As their very tortuous relationship with humans through the ages suggests, cats seem, if anything, more psychically connected to us than dogs.

Posting a call-out on my website to cat lovers, asking for any stories involving mindfulness on the part of their pets, I was inundated with stories of cats.

From Cape Town, South Africa, Belinda Joubert tells the story of how one day she was experiencing 'the dark hour of the soul' and was sitting in front of her computer screen, crying. Suddenly, her Russian blue cat, Victory, appeared:

> He jumped on my desk, sat on my keyboard and looked me straight in the eyes with those soft but intense green eyes. What happened next was mind blowing. Victory took both his front paws and he touched my cheeks; then, while keeping his paws on my face, he bent forward and put his head on my nose as if he was blessing me. I felt an intense love that he transferred

to me and it was as if I was given a soul-shot of inspiration. His kind act was filled with pure love and compassion and it felt as if God was somehow there.

A different story is shared by a reader from Brazil: 'When my son came home in the middle of the night to pack his things after leaving college, the male cat living with me at the time woke me by batting me with his paw, then getting me to follow him out to the front door so that I could hug my silent son goodbye for what was to be the last time.'

The experiences of many cat lovers confirm accounts, like Belinda's, of cats appearing from nowhere to offer comfort to human companions in their hour of need. Cats paying particular attention to a person's body part, which later turned out to be diseased. And cats going out to the gate to wait for their people to come home, even when they have been away for months and had, themselves, not known exactly when they'd be returning.

Not long ago I heard the story of neighbours who were asked to take care of a cat whose owners had recently retired and were travelling overseas for an extended period. The owners hadn't confirmed the date of their return home—they could be away for two months, maybe three. They wanted to take their time and not feel boxed in by an inflexible timetable.

On the day they returned, having had no contact with their neighbours, they discovered fresh milk in the fridge, bread on the counter and flowers on the table. How had their cat-sitting neighbours known?

That morning, for the first time ever, their neighbour later reported, their friends' cat had walked down the driveway and spent a long time at the kerb, facing up the road. This was such uncharacteristic behaviour, they suspected it could mean only one thing.

I will be sharing other intriguing stories during the course of this book. And most cat owners will not be especially surprised by any of them. We may not have personally experienced each one of these things, but we've observed enough similar or other examples of feline perceptiveness to know that cats, like dogs, seem to operate on a level of knowingness that runs behind or beyond ordinary cognition.

That being the case, why has such a massive gulf between scientific thought and everyday experience opened up in the past few hundred years?

WESTERN 'ENLIGHTENMENT': ANIMALS LACK CONSCIOUSNESS

It is a curious paradox that since the Western 'Enlightenment', scientists and philosophers have been the most strident voices in denying that most conscious beings on earth are, in fact, conscious.

From the late seventeenth century there was a new era in the Western world, with an emphasis on reason and empirical evidence. The Catholic Church was no longer regarded as the source of wisdom on all things and, instead, scientists were the new thought leaders when it came to the natural and material world.

René Descartes—of 'I think therefore I am' fame—was one of the leading figures in the scientific revolution, and his ideas about animal sentience, revealed in a letter to the Marquess of Newcastle in 1646, probably reflected the general views of scientists of his day:

... the reason why animals do not speak as we do is not that they lack the organs but that they have no thoughts. It cannot be said that they speak to each other and that we cannot understand them; because since dogs and some other animals express their passions to us, they would express their thoughts also if they had any ... if they thought as we do, they would have an immortal soul like us. This is unlikely, because there is no reason to believe it of some animals without believing it of all, and many of them such as oysters and sponges are too imperfect for this to be credible.[12]

Descartes' view that animals possessed the organs to speak was ignorant of basic biology. Even our closest relatives, primates, lack the connective ability to control their vocal chords to anything like the extent that we can.

As for the ideas that animals are essentially void of all thought, or that what is true of one species must automatically be true of them all, they would be laughable if it wasn't for the fact that they became scientific orthodoxy.

In particular, the notion that animals didn't possess 'an immortal soul like us' gave scientists, and the wider community, a carte blanche to treat them as they wished, because they were only, after all, robotic automatons.

Descartes himself used to conduct live vivisections of dogs, using blades to cut open their bodies while describing the organs within, all the time dismissing their agonised howling as mere reflex signifying nothing. In today's world he would be hauled before a court on charges of animal cruelty. But in his mind, that idea would have been as absurd as being cruel to an iPhone. Animals had no thought, no intelligence, no language and no soul: scientifically, as well as spiritually, they were zeros.

If the perspective of seventeenth-century scientists had evolved, we may have been able to leave an era of scarcely believable pitilessness and ignorance well behind us. But instead, not only did this view of the absence of animal consciousness remain powerful and enduring, it also came to be incorporated in the doctrine of materialism—an approach that has had the most diminishing consequences for the wellbeing of pets and other beings, including ourselves.

MOVING AWAY FROM A HUMAN-CENTRIC VIEW

Materialism suggests that if something isn't matter, or cannot be directly observed impacting on matter, then it doesn't exist. Behaviourists working from this perspective have long taken the view that we should make no assumptions that animals can think and feel, unless these things can be validated in repeatable, measurable experiments designed by humans.

For example, a dog that rushes towards you when you return home at the end of the day, wagging his tail, should not be assumed to be expressing happiness at seeing you. This may merely be the conditioned reflex of a furry-faced robot anticipating its next meal. The cat that settles on your lap in the evening, or the parrot that sidles up to you on the sofa and leans his head against your cheek, is not necessarily enjoying a moment of closeness with you. Those fluffy or feathery automatons could simply be seeking warmth. It is unscientific and, worst of all crimes, anthropomorphic, to project thoughts and feelings onto animals when their mind is unknowable.

Making no assumptions may be sensible and scientific, but behaviourists have long taken matters a step further, *insisting* that animals have no thoughts and feelings. They have also applied human-centric notions of communication and intelligence to concretise their positions. Carl Safina explains how materialism contradicts other scientific approaches in his book, *Beyond Words: What animals think and feel*:

... because we cannot converse with other animals, animal behaviourists threw up their hands, saying we can't know if they think or feel, and we should assume they cannot. Human behaviourists—Freud comes to mind—suffer no such self-straitjacketing. They try to tell you what you don't realize you are thinking. What you are feeling that you haven't verbalized. This double standard is peculiar, don't you think? On the one hand, you have professionals saying that we can't know whether other animals think because they're not using words, yet different professionals say that words can't explain what humans really think.[13]

As a species, we ignore the sentience of other beings because they don't speak a language we can easily understand. For centuries it has been assumed that animals can speak no language at all, and further assumed that they lack the intelligence and capacity to do so. The chain of assumptions continues: given that language and cognition go hand in hand, other animals must not be capable of developed thought and reasoning. How can one plan or strategise without words to think? Emotional maturity is also impossible without intellectual development. And as for the development of moral reasoning—concepts like fairness, altruism and compassion—well, forget it. Without language, such elevated conceptualisation is out of the question.

These assumptions are not only important. They are the basis on which our society has decided that the chasm dividing humans from other species is so great it is reasonable to regard them as mere units of production, expendable as any other non-sentient resource such as oil, iron ore and paper.

But do these assumptions, which provide the framework for our treatment of animals, really stand up to scrutiny?

The most telling evidence of our human-centric world view is the fact that we have made so little effort to understand if and how the most populous beings on earth communicate, and whether it's true that complex language necessarily goes hand in hand with moral reasoning and emotional development. Only recently have researchers started to take these subjects seriously. And their initial findings, some of which are summarised in the next chapter, suggest that an intriguing convergence is beginning to take place between scientific outliers in the West, and the wisdom traditions of the East. It is a convergence that not only has the potential to profoundly shift the way that humans interact with other beings, but also deepens our confidence in the significant purpose we can serve in helping develop the inner lives of our pets.

HOW THE WORLD LOOKS, SOUNDS AND SMELLS DIFFERENT TO OUR PETS

We share the same world as our pets, yet we do not perceive the same reality.

Both cats and dogs have only 20 per cent of the cone photoreceptor cells of humans, meaning they can only see the colours blue and yellow. All other colours are shades of grey. Dogs and cats also can't focus on far distant objects. If any of us woke up one morning with the vision of our pet, we'd be visiting the optician immediately. The night vision of both dogs and cats is better than ours, however, probably out of evolutionary necessity.

The world also sounds different to cats and dogs. The hearing range of cats reaches an impressive two octaves higher than our own into ultrasound, with the noises made by bats and rodents as clearly audible to them as the shrieks of children are to us.

Human noses have around five million olfactory receptors, enabling us to sense odours. Cats have around ten to fourteen times this number while dogs have between 150 and 300 million receptors, making dogs' sense of smell a thousand times more acute than ours. It is for exactly these reasons that detector dogs are used by Australian Border Force, and trained as Diabetic Alert Dogs as well as Seizure Alert Dogs for people living with epilepsy. In the United Kingdom, pioneering trials are being held to identify if Medical Detection Dogs can help in the early detection of a variety of cancers—including prostate, breast and others—offering a very different form of 'lab test'.

Most animals, including cats and dogs, have an additional olfactory system, the vomeronasal organ (VNO), which falls somewhere between smell and taste. When they pause over a scent of interest, pulling their top lip upwards and opening their mouths partially for a few seconds, this smell/taste response is kicking in.

The abilities of our pets to hear and smell by far outstrips our own. And other animals have extraordinary perceptual ranges quite different from us. Cetaceans, like dolphins, actually 'see' in 3D using echolocation. Elephants communicate in a bass rumble which we can't hear, but may feel, right in the solar plexus, if we happen to be standing nearby.

Most humans are strongly visual beings. We need to remember that what we see is a lot less vivid to our pets—and that they can hear and smell a much more engaging reality than we are ever aware of.

CHAPTER TWO

ANIMALS ARE CONSCIOUS BEINGS TOO

Dr Irene M. Pepperberg with Alex, the African grey parrot. 'Scientifically speaking, the single greatest lesson Alex taught me, taught all of us, is that animal minds are a great deal more like human minds than the vast majority of behavioural scientists believed—or, more importantly, were even prepared to concede, might be remotely possible.'

ANIMAL CONSCIOUSNESS AND COMMUNICATION are such new fields of formal study that there are only small groups of researchers undertaking research in the area. The researchers have tended to focus on species of more social mammals such as whales, wolves, primates and elephants, where a lot of communication goes on the whole time. And the results of the studies have been extraordinary.

To start with a very familiar species, in *The Genius of Dogs: How dogs are smarter than you think*, canine cognition researchers Professor Brian Hare and Vanessa Woods show that there is a lot more to barking than most humans realise. Dogs subtly alter their barking to have different meanings in different contexts. While most people can tell the difference between playful barking and aggressive barking, peoples' ability to discriminate between different dogs that are barking, and what their growls or barks signify, is found to be extremely limited. Hare and Woods conclude: 'we know very little about the vocal behavior of dogs'.[1] This is an extraordinary finding, given that our lives have been so closely entwined with theirs for the past 15,000 years!

More accurate than saying that animals don't have language could be the admission that we have never properly studied how they communicate. Today's zoologists will confirm that elephants have a repertoire of over 100 gestures to signal to each other on a wide range of matters. They always greet each other, and the way they do so denotes the quality of their relationship, with the most important relationships generating the greatest excitement.

Elephants use not only non-verbal gestures but also low frequency sounds, inaudible to humans, which travel over several kilometres, to keep in touch with each other. If a group of elephants is attacked by poachers, other groups some distance away immediately know about it and behave in a traumatised way.

One of the most haunting stories related by Carl Safina in his outstanding book *Beyond Words: What animals think and feel*, is that of the researcher who played a recording of an elephant who had died, through a speaker in the bush. The family of the dead elephant was distraught, calling out for their sister and mother, searching in vain for her. Her daughter called out for her for days afterwards. 'The researchers,' says Safina, 'never again did such a thing.'[2]

Just like us, elephants can communicate verbally to some extent. They even recognise one another's voices.

Above and beyond the visible, non-verbal signing, and the audible and inaudible vocalisation, however, elephants seem to use another level of communication, the same one that enables dogs—and cats, horses, birds and no doubt others—to perceive that their owners are on their way home.

An example is the orphaned elephants rescued by the David Sheldrick Wildlife Trust in Kenya, who are nurtured through their early years before being taken to the Tsavo National Park to join others like them, released into the bush years earlier.

The transition from protected sanctuary to their natural habitat is huge. But after decades of having repeated this process, Daphne Sheldrick has observed how other former orphans, now grown up and living in the wild, emerge from the bush to greet the newcomers and make them feel welcome. 'Daphne Sheldrick insists that the elephants in Tsavo know when a new group of orphans is headed there in trucks on the road from Nairobi. She claims that free-living grown-ups come from the bush, ready to meet young new orphans when they arrive. She calls it "telepathy." I filed her claim in my mind's "unlikely stories" bin. But that bin gets cluttered; there are many "unlikely" stories about elephants.'[3]

PRIMATE SIGNERS WHO UNDERSTAND ENGLISH

Moving closer to our own species, primates are known to use vocalisations, with different species of monkey using specific sounds—words—to denote specific animals and their status, from 'snake' and 'baboon' to 'unfamiliar human' and 'dominant monkey'. Some use a form of syntax to denote how far away a particular threat may be. Vervet monkeys have been known to cry out 'leopard!' if their troop is being overwhelmed by another, sending their attackers into the trees through the use of deliberate miscommunication. A tactic not unknown in corporate boardrooms today.

Of all the primates to be studied at close quarters, Koko the gorilla is one of the most famous. Born in San Francisco Zoo in 1971 before coming into the care of Francine 'Penny' Patterson, who was undertaking a PhD in Psychology at Stanford University, Koko is a female Western Lowland gorilla who has learned a large number of hand signs from a modified version of American Sign Language, and understands about 2000 words in English. Patterson has written many reports, including several books, explaining Koko's use of language. Predictably, these findings have been rebutted by sceptics in the scientific community, claiming that Koko doesn't understand the signs she is using, that any meaning attributed to her signing is projected by humans and that any correct answers she gives are in the manner of Clever Hans, a horse at the turn of the last century who could supposedly count, tell the time and so on, when in reality he was only responding to the leaked, non-verbal cues of his owner.

But there is a wealth of evidence to the contrary. Koko has displayed humour in her communications and has also made deliberately deceptive statements when it suited her agenda. She has also invented phrases—having not been taught the word 'ring' she came up, on her own, with 'finger bracelet'.

Washoe, the chimpanzee, originally captured by the United States Air Force for use on the space program, but who was, instead, brought up by Allen and Beatrix Gardner in Washoe County, Nevada, was the first primate to learn American Sign Language. She not only demonstrated her capacity to do so, but also an awareness of herself and others that could be humbling. When novice signers came to work with her, she would slow down her rate of signing to accommodate them.

There are many reports and resources about Washoe available online. The account that really touched me was her interest in the pregnancy of a research assistant. Touching her belly, she signed 'baby'. When the assistant had a miscarriage, she decided she had to tell Washoe what had happened, as Washoe had lost her own babies in the past. She signed, 'My baby died.' At this, Washoe met her eyes directly and signed 'cry', touching her cheek just below her eye. Later that day, she didn't want the research assistant to leave work, signing, 'Please person hug'—thereby demonstrating not only her understanding and empathy, but also extending a heartfelt compassion.[4]

TALKING AND TELEPATHY: AFRICAN GREY PARROTS

Animals can even speak English! Alex, an African grey parrot, is the only bird to have received an obituary in both *The New York Times* and *The Economist*, because he learned scores of words and showed he understood what they meant.[5] Alex could identify over 50 objects, distinguish a variety of colours and shapes, and demonstrate an understanding of concepts like bigger and smaller, over and under again. (You can watch this fascinating process yourself on YouTube: Alex—One of the smartest parrots ever.)

Just as was the case with Koko the gorilla, no sooner were reports published than a wave of scientific scepticism followed. Alex didn't understand what he said, said some. Just because he said words didn't mean he could use syntax, said others. Clever Hans was once again invoked, even though Alex was able to answer similar questions when asked by a variety of researchers.

Dr Irene M. Pepperberg, the MIT and Harvard trained scientist who led the initiative to explore language and intelligence with Alex, describes how for 30 years she felt she had been banging her head against a wall—no matter what evidence she was able to produce to demonstrate that Alex could cognise and communicate in English, the evidence was dismissed by scientists who had already decided that animals can't think, whatever the facts of the matter.

In her book, *Alex and Me*, Pepperberg writes:

Scientifically speaking, the single greatest lesson Alex taught me, taught all of us, is that animal minds are a great deal more like human minds than the vast majority of behavioural scientists believed—or, more importantly, were even prepared to concede might be remotely possible ... Alex taught us how little we know about animal minds and how much more there is to discover. This insight has profound implications, philosophically, sociologically, and practically. It affects our view of the species *Homo sapiens* and its place in nature.[6]

Pepperberg's pioneering work has been followed up by others with African grey parrots, who are widely acknowledged to be among the quickest learners in the parrot world. Growing up in Africa, I knew several people who kept them as pets and I used to love my interactions with them. I would have been thrilled to offer a home to an African grey myself but my parents wouldn't allow it, because the parrots' life expectancy is an average 40 to 60 years. There was never any doubt in my mind that I was interacting with a sharp, intriguing and often somewhat mischievous intelligence that went well beyond whatever pidgin interaction we might be having.

As a boy who hand-reared a number of cockatiels, I also never doubted the capacity of parrots to feel a wide range of emotions. The way that many parrots, like some other birds, mate for life, gives rise to one of the most poignant of these. A friend told me that one of the most heart-rending sights he ever encountered in the bird world was a pet parrot who had an open wound on her featherless chest. The parrot's owner told my friend how the parrot had recently lost her mate. In the days and weeks since, she had pulled every feather out of her chest and even pecked into her own skin, such was her grief.

An especially intriguing illustration of parrots' intelligence, telepathy and ability to learn English is provided by Aimée Morgana, a New York based artist who had an African grey parrot called N'kisi. What makes parrots especially interesting to study, from a telepathic perspective, is that they are literally able to give voice to their reactions about what people are planning, thinking and feeling. In Morgana's case, such was the closeness of her relationship with her parrot that N'kisi used to regularly comment on things, such as who she was about to call when she picked up the phone, or images she might be looking at on a TV screen that he couldn't see—'Don't fall down', when a man was scarily perched on a girder high on a skyscraper. Most remarkably, N'kisi, who shared Morgana's bedroom, would even comment on what she was dreaming. 'You gotta push the button,' he said, waking her up once, when she was dreaming about working with an audio tape deck.

After reading Rupert Sheldrake's book, *Dogs That Know When Their Owners Are Coming Home*,[7] Morgana contacted Sheldrake, who proposed a study to see if N'kisi's telepathic skills could be objectively established. Sheldrake designed a trial, during which Morgana looked at many different photographs of objects N'kisi knew about, in a randomised, controlled experiment, while N'kisi, on a different floor of the building, was simultaneously filmed. Out of 71 items, he correctly identified 23—a result that is way above chance and highly significant statistically.[8] Rupert Sheldrake reports more on this and many other studies in his intriguing book, *The Sense of Being Stared At: and other aspects of the extended mind*, and you can find a video of the experiment on my blog at: davidmichie.com/do-animals-use-telepathy-to-communicate-intriguing-video-evidence/.

ALTRUISM AND COMPASSION: DEFINING QUALITIES OF A SPIRITUAL LIFE

Some animals can communicate with other than their own species. The handful of primates and parrots who can recognise and respond appropriately to English words probably represents a handful more than the humans who can recognise and vocalise appropriately in West Lowland gorilla or African grey parrot.

Beyond this, telepathy is a recurring if not routine element in animal communication for which there is no human counterpart. While many of us may have experienced telepathic messages, or at least know others who have, it is not an ongoing part of our repertoire. We communicate verbally and non-verbally, but if we ever had the ability to communicate in more subtle ways, it seems to have become obscured beneath the waves of thought and agitation in our minds.

It is my own view that intuition and telepathy are subtle, natural phenomena, but that the minds of most people have become so noisy, for so many generations, that as a species we have largely forgotten this capability.

If we are willing to be open, we discover that not only language but also empathy and compassion are demonstrated by a wide range of creatures. Far from animals lacking the kinds of qualities we might identify as necessary for a spiritual life, what we are discovering is that it is we, humans, who have been lacking. Despite sharing our planet for so long with so many other sentient beings, it is only in the last twenty or so years that we have made any properly considered attempts to understand how they communicate, think and feel.

In the last chapter we looked at several examples of dogs and cats who have shown very high levels of awareness, understanding, compassion, planning and intelligence—like the dog who smashed a window to alert passers-by to his sick owner; the golden retriever who woke his people to warn them about a fire; the Russian blue who arrived from nowhere to comfort her owner in the most extraordinary way. These are only a few of the very many examples people have shared with me. Many more are documented in books such as Jennifer Skiff's delightful *The Divinity of Dogs*. Recently I was told a story from Tasmania involving a dog who lived with Mum, Dad and the kids in a regular household. Every morning the father would leave home and walk down to the harbour to catch a ferry into work. One morning, about twenty minutes after he'd left for the day, the dog suddenly became very distressed, barking and scratching frantically at the back door. The mother let him out, but that wasn't enough—the dog ran to the gate and barked urgently for her to follow. So unusual was the dog's behaviour, and so compelling, that she followed it to the gate and outside, into the street, taking the same route as her husband did every morning. Shortly before reaching the ferry terminal, they discovered her husband lying on the ground. He had just suffered a massive heart attack. The wife was able to summon help quickly and the man's life was saved. How might one describe the behaviour of the dog, if not that of effective and compassionate action based on powerful extra-sensory perception?

Such attributes are by no means limited to dogs and cats. Readers have shared many other wonderful stories with me. Marjolijne de Groot, from Belgium, told me about her horse, Vasco:

> When my father passed away, for days long I felt numb, in a sort of shell. Somebody told me I had to go and ride, that it would do me good. Now my horse is this typical 'seeing ghosts' when we ride in the forest, so you always have to be very alert because anything will make him jump around. But not that week! I only noticed it afterwards. I saddled him, went into the forest every day, he was walking me, not the other way around. He was as nice and calm as never before. No jumping around, no fear of leaves, reflections in the water ... he was just simply superb and caring. When I started to feel better and came out of that mourning, he returned to his old self. That is when I noticed what he had done for me for a week: he had been taking care of me, he felt I was not ok and he decided that he had to protect me.

Another tale of compassion involves Lulu, the pot-bellied pig, who saved the life of her owner, Jo Anne Altsman, when Jo Anne suffered a heart attack while on holiday in Pennsylvania. Seeing her owner unconscious and in desperate need of help, Lulu managed to get out of the house and through the gate, and ran into the street where she lay down in the middle of the road. She was ignored by several vehicles before a man finally got out of his car to check she wasn't hurt. Lulu led the man back to the house and her unconscious owner. The man dialled 911 to summon help and Jo Anne lived to tell the tale.[9]

One quality, only recently investigated by researchers, but which some animals have been shown to possess, is a sense of fairness. Frans de Waal, who has spent much of his career studying primates, and has been named one of *Time* magazine's 100 Most Influential People, explains: 'A few years ago, we demonstrated that primates will happily perform a task for cucumber slices until they see others getting grapes, which taste so much better. The cucumber eaters become agitated, throw down their veggies, and go on strike. A perfectly fine food has become unpalatable as a result of seeing a companion get something better.'[10]

The same experiment has been repeated with other species, including dogs, who will similarly 'go on strike' if another dog is rewarded for a trick it was performing without expectation of reward. Fairness and equivalency are among the cognitive capabilities thought to be well beyond the scope of beings without the language to achieve intellectual development. New studies prove otherwise.

While many pet lovers have experienced the empathy and compassion shown by their furry and feathery friends, even outside the context of such relationships these qualities can be repeatedly observed.

Jane Goodall, renowned primatologist and ethologist, notes how even though chimpanzees and bonobos can't swim, they have made 'heroic efforts' to save companions from drowning. An eight-year-old American boy who fell into the ape pit at Brookfield Zoo, and was knocked unconscious, was gently lifted by Binti Jua, a female gorilla, who took him to the door of her enclosure and handed him over to her keepers.[11]

Not so long ago, a video was doing the rounds on social media, showing a monkey in India rescuing another monkey who had fallen unconscious onto the rails at a train station, after being electrocuted.

While crowds of commuters stood on the platforms recording the whole thing on their mobile phones, the monkey dragged his mate off the rails, tried to shake him awake, and dunked him in a water channel, not stopping in his efforts until the other monkey came back to consciousness.[12]

The idea that empathy is the preserve of primates has been overturned by research at the University of Chicago, where neuroscientist Peggy Mason showed that rats would work to free other rats who were trapped in a container, even when there was no reward. Says Mason: 'Helping is our evolutionary inheritance. Our study suggests that we don't have to cognitively decide to help an individual in distress; rather, we just have to let our animal selves express themselves.'[13]

What a refreshingly bold assertion from a researcher—that altruism, far from being a cherished virtue exclusive to humans, is actually a virtue shared by all sentient beings!

Even fish should form a part of our circle of compassion. Recent research by Dr Caitlin Newport of the University of Oxford shows that fish are able to recognise human faces.[14] The cognitive complexity of fish comes as a surprise to many people—not only do fish think and feel, they also cooperate, can choose to reconcile, and demonstrate other unexpected mental capabilities.[15] Dr Victoria Braithwaite, renowned fish biologist, wrote a book *Do Fish Feel Pain?*, in which she concluded: 'I have argued that there is as much evidence that fish feel pain and suffer as there is for birds and mammals—and more than there is for human neonates and preterm babies.'[16]

THE CAMBRIDGE DECLARATION

In recent years, the work of pioneering animal cognitive scientists and others has done much to open our minds to animal sentience. A new generation of scientists, unfettered by the dogma of behaviourism, is able to recognise the absurdity of applying contrived human yardsticks, and is more eager to study animals on their own terms.

The implications of quantum science have also begun to impact on our thinking about consciousness and communication. There is a growing recognition that not only is matter *not* the only thing that exists, but there is hardly any of it! Things aren't as solid as was once believed. Matter may also be expressed as energy—and that notion opens up a whole new dimension of possibilities that may help explain what, until recently, has been inexplicable: the illusion of subject and object; the impact of the observer on the observed; and the phenomenon of non-locality. These concepts blow open the narrow assumptions of materialism and suggest the much more exciting possibilities of energetic fields in which concepts like telepathy, far from seeming unscientific, are an assumed fact. In the words of Albert Einstein:

> A human being . . . experiences himself, his thoughts and feelings as something separated from the rest—a kind of optical illusion of his consciousness. This delusion is a kind of prison for us, restricting us to our personal desires and to affection for a few persons nearest to us. Our task must be to free ourselves from this prison by widening our circle of understanding and compassion to embrace all living creatures and the whole of nature in its beauty.[17]

Alternatively, as His Holiness the Dalai Lama puts it: 'True happiness comes not from a limited concern for one's own wellbeing, or that of those one feels close to, but from developing love and compassion for all sentient beings.'[18]

One of the most encouraging developments for an official recognition of animal sentience came about in July 2012 with the proclamation of The Cambridge Declaration. Some of the world's most eminent scientists, with Stephen Hawking as guest of honour, affirmed that humans are not the only beings to experience consciousness. The key part of the declaration reads as follows:

> We declare the following: 'The absence of a neocortex does not appear to preclude an organism from experiencing affective states. Convergent evidence indicates that non-human animals have the neuroanatomical, neurochemical, and neurophysiological substrates of conscious states along with the capacity to exhibit intentional behaviors. Consequently, the weight of evidence indicates that humans are not unique in possessing the neurological substrates that generate consciousness. Nonhuman animals, including all mammals and birds, and many other creatures, including octopuses, also possess these neurological substrates.'[19]

It may have taken a long time to get there, but Western scientists and Eastern masters of consciousness are now making their way to the same page: all animals, human and non-human, are conscious. We all possess minds. Acceptance of this fact provides the basis for the main subject of this book: how best to apply the consciousness possessed by our pets, as well as ourselves, for the most mutually beneficial outcome?

CLOSE TO NATURE: HUMAN SOCIETIES WHERE TELEPATHY IS COMMONPLACE

Could it be the case that, instead of telepathy being some kind of weird, paranormal phenomenon accepted only by the gullible, it is, rather, a quite natural phenomenon which is no longer accessible to us because our minds are simply too damned busy?

When we look at pre-literate human societies, we discover the same co-existence of telepathic communication with quieter minds that seems to abide in animals. In *The Lost World of the Kalahari*, Laurens van der Post, the Afrikaans philosopher, psychologist and a colleague of Jung's, tells the story of how, in 1955, he was commissioned by the BBC to make a documentary about living with the Bushmen, or San people, as they are now known. Accompanying a group on a hunt, during which they killed an eland—a large antelope—he asked a Bushman called Dabe how he thought his people would react to the successful kill. Dabe told him that his people already knew. Uncertain how to take this, Van der Post asked him what he meant. Dabe, who had once accompanied a white man into the city and seen a telegraph wire being operated, tapped his chest and said, 'We bushmen have a wire here that brings us news.' Sure enough, as they approached camp, they could hear the gathered villagers singing 'The Eland Song'.[20]

A Professor of Anthropology and Anglican clergyman, Adolphus Elkin, spent a great deal of time meticulously observing Aboriginal people in the remote Kimberley ranges of Western Australia, before many of them had had much contact with the outside world. He collected a large number of reports on psychic phenomena, including telepathy over very long distances, healing, seeing spirits and out of body experiences. Elkin attributed these qualities to the quiet and solitude of the bush, openness to experience and a sense of timelessness.[21]

To find evidence that a quieter and more mindful life, living close to nature, gives rise to psychic phenomena, we don't necessarily need to go back in time. I was talking to a friend about this subject, and he told me about something he experienced last year when pony trekking in Mongolia. Part of a group of sixteen, including several rugged Europeans, they were discussing how it was time to find a place to settle late one afternoon, when one of the Mongolians remembered a farm he'd visited in the past where they might find some shelter. The group headed in that direction, eventually coming to a few wooden buildings in the middle of nowhere.

My friend joined the leader of the trek who walked towards the buildings to ask the farmer's permission to stay. What he found, after an elderly woman showed them into the modest family dwelling, astonished him: there was an abundance of freshly made dumplings on the table and a large pot of stew on the fire. Not only were the trekkers welcome to stay the night, the woman had prepared them dinner.

How had she known?

The woman smiled with a shrug when asked the question. On waking up that morning, she said, she had 'seen' a group of sixteen people coming over the mountain that afternoon, including several 'big foreign men'. So she had made them a meal.

No need for emails, Wi-Fi or Airbnb!

CHAPTER THREE

GUIDING PRINCIPLES

Pixel, the three-year-old rescue greyhound, loves long naps, playing with her furry siblings and exploring the neighbourhood on her evening strolls. ALEX CEARNS/HOUNDSTOOTH STUDIO

WHAT ARE THE KEY principles offered by Tibetan Buddhism to guide us in the way we can best help our pets in life, as well as through death? In this chapter I outline what I believe to be the most relevant concepts. Although presented in summary form, each principle is profound in its implications.

Readers who would like to explore Tibetan Buddhism in more detail may do so in my books *Buddhism For Busy People*, which provides an overview, and *Enlightenment To Go*, which offers more detailed suggestions on how to integrate Buddha's teachings—collectively known as the Dharma—into the fabric of everyday life.

ALL BEINGS—ANIMAL AND HUMAN—HAVE A MIND

In Tibetan Buddhism, all sentient beings are known as 'sem chens', which translates as 'mind havers'. There is no difference between humans and other animals in this regard.

Tibetan Buddhism is not asserting that cockroaches, birds or even our beloved dog are intellectually equivalent to us. The 'mind' being referred to here is much more subtle than that.

Part of the challenge of understanding Buddhism in the West is the sparseness of our language when translating terms from Sanskrit or Pali. In the same way that some languages are said to have many different words for snow, because subtle distinctions are so self-evident to those who are immersed in that particular world, so too, when translating words that describe different aspects of consciousness into English, we sometimes have to make do with only rough approximations.

The 'mind' we all share does not refer to sensory perception, intellect, memory, personality or many of the other elements that comprise the typical Western description of mind. It refers to a more subtle phenomenon: 'a formless continuum of clarity and cognition'.

'Formless', because mind is not material. We can't point to anything tangible and say 'that is mind'.

'Continuum' refers to the energetic continuity in our experience of mind, with one mind moment constantly following another, like the flow of a river. Mind is not static—it has a dynamic quality. 'Continuum' describes the way that each mind moment arises as a result of a previous mind moment, not in a linear way—any glimpse of our own mind will soon establish that—but as an effect of a previously created cause.

'Clarity' describes another aspect of mind—how it is capable of reflecting, perceiving and experiencing whatever arises. Buddhist teachers use several different analogies to illustrate this quality. The sky is one such metaphor, with every thought, perception or sensation like a cloud that passes through it. We shouldn't confuse the clouds for the sky. We are not our thoughts. Thoughts, beliefs, interpretations all arise, abide and pass through our mind without remaining. Not a single thought you've ever had is in your mind as you read this sentence, now. Thoughts have no permanence, and cannot remain in our mind unless we engage them with our attention.

The discovery that we are not our thoughts, that we can choose to engage, or not engage with thoughts, and that we can learn to become observers of our thoughts rather than their victims is one of the most life-enhancing skills any of us can develop. I have written about this extensively in my book *Why Mindfulness Is Better Than Chocolate*.

'Cognition' is the ability to perceive and understand. The word encompasses all elements of mental activity, including our capacity to sense, interpret, think, remember, plan, visualise and so on. As experiences arise, enabled by the clarity of mind, its cognitive function is what we use to make sense of those experiences.

Whether we are human, cat, pigeon or alpaca, each one of us has a mind that may be described as a formless continuum of clarity and cognition.

ALL BEINGS—ANIMAL AND HUMAN—HAVE BUDDHA POTENTIAL

If we have a mind, we have the potential to become enlightened. The Tibetan Buddhist view is that ultimately we all will become enlightened. Our enlightenment is possible because each one of us possesses some capacity for love, compassion and other virtuous qualities which, through continuous development, become a cause for Buddhahood.

Whether or not we make the choices that propel us along this path is, of course, up to us. Interestingly, many of the behaviours which take us in a positive direction share much with those emphasised in other major traditions: pleasures of the material world are unreliable and short-lived, whereas love and compassion for others are our most enduring sources of wellbeing; in giving, we receive; action is most effective when founded on contemplation. Whether we act from religious or secular convictions, whenever we create positive causes, there can only be positive effects.

When considering our treatment of animals, especially our pets, it is helpful to cultivate an underlying reverence for the fact that we are dealing with beings who have just as much Buddha potential as we do. And given that the process of enlightenment may be a long one, who is to say that our dog or cat won't get there ahead of us?

The Buddhist sage, Shantideva, who wrote what was effectively the world's first self-help book back in the eighth century (*A Guide to the Bodhisattva's Way of Life*), described a single human lifetime as being like a flash of lightning in the sky, it is so transient. What if the being who is currently our pet budgie is merely using up some negative karma before manifesting as an extraordinary human being—and perhaps as our mother or father in its next lifetime? Who is to say that our dog doesn't possess the potential to achieve enlightenment well before we do? We may be human in this lifetime—believed to be the optimal form in which to create the causes for our enlightenment. But the future is uncertain. Just as our own actions will propel us in a particular direction, so, too, our dog's. It is both humbling and entirely realistic to keep our minds open to the reality that just because we relate to other beings in a specific form right now, this will not always be so.

As pet lovers, we have both the opportunity, as well as the responsibility, to help our close companions create the causes that will help actualise their Buddha potential. Their journey through this particular life is something we can do much to enhance. This is the basis of many of the practices proposed in this book.

EACH OF US ATTACHES THE HIGHEST VALUE TO OUR OWN LIFE

The most precious thing to each of us is being alive. We have no problem agreeing with this conceptually, but on an everyday level it's easy to lose sight of the fact that life is both transient and extremely precious. We tend to assume we will live to a ripe old age, even though we have no reason to do so. How often do we hear people say, 'If only it was Friday', on a Monday or Tuesday, thereby wishing away precious time from a life that may be a lot shorter than they suppose?

As a society we often defer our potential for fulfilment and joy until some mythical time in the future—the 'I'll be happy when . . .' syndrome. *When* we have met our life partner, or had children, or *when* the children have left home, or *when* we have achieved some particular goal—even if that is only the end of our working life.

There is no greater wake-up call than a road accident or medical emergency to alert us to the true value of our life. Buddhists are encouraged to meditate regularly on the stark certainty of our own death. This is not out of morbid introspection, but for the opposite reason. It is only when we face our own death that we truly know how to live. Only when we experience a vivid awareness of the preciousness of each day may we be truly present to the here and now, and prioritise what and who is important to us.

As pet lovers, we need to take care not to impose on animal companions our tendency to put off fulfilment to the future. We should certainly make no assumptions about longevity when it comes to beings whose lives are, in most cases, only a tiny fraction the length of our own. Life is for living, here and now. This may be as good as it gets. We may want to procrastinate about taking the dog for a walk because the weather forecast is better tomorrow. But how does that help our canine friend make the most of today? Brushing the cat for the umpteenth time may seem a chore—but if we never had the chance to do it again, would we take more care to make that special connection?

Valuing the preciousness of each moment of life leads us to the sanctity of life itself. We have no reason to assume that an animal's life is any less valuable to that animal than our own life is to us. Observing how animals behave when they know their life is under threat tells us all we need to know about the value which they attach to it: mothers will fight to their last breath to defend their children. Animals who sense that their lives are in danger will go to extreme lengths to survive.

If we were to be chased across a vast plain by giants wielding canisters of toxic gas, we would probably behave no differently from the terrified cockroach, scrambling and defecating across the kitchen floor as it searches in desperation for safe refuge.

Attaching no value at all to life is, if anything, uniquely human. There is no evidence of suicide among other sentient beings. You rarely find self-harm among animals that live in the wild. And yet self-destructive behaviour of varying kinds is among the rising challenges facing health services throughout the developed world.

The Buddhist view is that all sentient beings cherish their own life above all else. This is why we strive to protect the lives of others. So important is this principle that abandoning killing is the first—and only required—vow taken upon becoming a Buddhist.

EACH ONE OF US WANTS HAPPINESS AND TO AVOID DISSATISFACTION

It may seem an obvious point that all beings are just the same as we are in wishing for happiness and to avoid suffering. But it is worth repeating because it is so often overlooked. We have no difficulty accepting that we can never have too much happiness. No matter how much we already enjoy, we wish for more. Just as we are eager to avoid the slightest dissatisfaction or suffering.

But in our pursuit of happiness, it can be easy to overlook or diminish the needs of others. In the words of Shantideva:

> First of all, I should make an effort
> To meditate upon the equality between self and others.
> I should protect all beings as I do myself
> Because we are all equal in wanting pleasure and not wanting
>   pain.

> When both myself and others
> Are similar in that we wish to be happy,
> What is so special about me?
> Why do I strive for my happiness alone?

And when both myself and others
Are similar in that we do not wish to suffer,
What is so special about me?
Why do I protect myself and not others?

We exert enormous control over the circumstances of our pets' lives. It is within our power to provide not only the most appealing and nutritious food, and most comfortable living conditions, but also to provide the outings, stimulation and affection that help them thrive.

This is an opportunity we should recognise because when we offer love, time and material support to others, we ourselves are the first beneficiaries. The Golden Rule, repeated in the major traditions down the ages, tells us that as we give, so we receive. For evidence of this, we need only think about the happiest people we know—they tend to be givers.

Giving is most often not about the grand gesture, or seeking recognition for our philanthropy. It is about the everyday moments when we respond to a meow at our heels, or a dog presenting us with his leash, or a bird fluffing out her feathers as she battles to keep warm. It is about doing sometimes quite small things with great love, embodying the life-enhancing wisdom that the deep sense of wellbeing we all yearn for comes from nurturing a benevolent connection to others.

OUR EXPERIENCE OF REALITY IS DETERMINED BY CAUSE AND EFFECT

As a society, we perpetuate the mistaken belief that the causes of our happiness or dissatisfaction are outside of us. Which is why we invest so much energy trying to get the externals of our lives just so: the home, family, career, toys, financial security, or whatever else we think form the ingredients of our personal recipe for happiness.

The reality is that these things, external to the mind are, at best, only contributing factors. The main cause of happiness arises from the mind itself. What we think about our circumstances is way more important than the circumstances themselves. Two people in much the same situation may feel very differently about it. The difference is how they interpret things. This is not only a Buddhist view—it is also the basis of cognitive behaviour therapy, one of the most widely used modalities in psychotherapy today.

Why is it that each of us sees the world in such a variety of different ways? Because of the way we have become accustomed to think. Or, as Buddhists would put it, because of karma.

On a moment by moment basis we are strengthening the patterns of thought and behaviour that shape the way we experience reality in the future. If we focus our attention on negativity, scarcity of resources, conflict and fear, our experience of the future will be an ever-magnified experience of these. Similarly, a focus on gratitude, compassion and open-heartedness develops our capacity for connectedness and joy. To enjoy happiness, we first create the causes for happiness.

As thoughts become translated into action, we interact with others in a way that influences not only our relationships with them, but also with others in times to come. We may catch a glimpse of cause and effect at work in a single lifetime. Negative and miserly people tend to become increasingly negative and miserly. Appreciative and open-hearted people become more spontaneously and naturally compassionate.

A more panoramic vantage point would enable us to see these patterns at work over lifetimes, with the energetic dynamic of karma propelling our consciousness into situations and relationships that are the effects of previously created causes. Taking care to create positive causes, or energetic imprints, and avoid negative ones, is the key to our future flourishing.

This is as true of our pets as it is of us. Buddha was once asked to summarise his teachings in just a few words. His reply was: 'Abandon harmfulness. Cultivate goodness. Subdue your mind.' Even if we can do nothing else, then avoiding negativity, and helping our pets avoid negativity, is a useful start. Whether it's attaching a bell collar round the neck of our hunter cat, or keeping our dog away from encounters that may trigger aggression, moment by moment we can become more aware of our pet's experience of reality and help shape their future experiences.

Helping our pet pooch create goodness may seem a tall order, but there is much we can do to imprint our pets' minds with powerfully positive images, words and behaviour. We should never underestimate the impact these activities may have on their consciousness—an impact that may only become manifest well into the future.

The example of the pigeon and Indian Buddhist master Vasabandhu is a fascinating one. Vasabandhu used to sit on a roof and daily recite a text called the *Abhidharmakosha*. Every day, he was overheard by a resident pigeon. So powerful were the imprints caused by hearing this precious text that when it died, the pigeon achieved human rebirth. One day Vasabandhu decided to check what had become of the pigeon, and through his clairvoyance he was able to see that it had been born as a child to a family in a nearby valley. He went to visit the family and after some years the child became a monk under his care, to whom Vasabandhu gave the name Lobpön Loden. Lobpön Loden in turn went on to become an expert on the *Abhidharmakosha*—it is said by some surpassing even the great Vasabandhu in his understanding of the text—and writing four commentaries on it. As it happens, my own precious lama, Geshe Acharya Thubten Loden, shares his name.

46

PETS ARE NOT IN OUR LIVES BY CHANCE

If someone asked how your pets came to be living with you, you may tell the story of a visit to the local cat refuge, or perhaps the adoption of a dog when his owner moved away, or the discovery of a bird that had fallen from her nest and would have died without your help. You would, in other words, be giving an answer according to conventional reality. A reality unique to you.

Many people going to the same cat refuge walked right past the feline with whom you are now so besotted. Others may have had no interest in adopting a dog, or may have been willing to act only as a temporary foster parent. And why did you walk under that particular tree at the precise moment that the baby bird, wrinkled and raucous, made her presence known?

As described above, the Buddhist view is that our experience of conventional reality is driven by cause and effect, or karma. This means there is nothing arbitrary in what we experience—and that the pets with whom we share our lives are not here by chance. From the countless billions of beings on planet earth alone, it is not through some random accident that we find ourselves sharing our homes and lives with only a specific few: it is because of the very strong connection we have to them.

The formless continuum of clarity and awareness, which is our mind, has threaded through numberless experiences of reality, like a string through an endless, beaded necklace of many colours. Some of these experiences have been positive, others quite the opposite—all depends on the karma we create.

In each lifetime we have interacted with many beings. We have had parents, siblings, members of our own species to whom we feel close, and those with whom we are in competition or conflict. Our relationship with the being who currently sits at our feet or on our shoulder may have been astonishingly different in a previous lifetime. Or even at a different time in this one. But certain conditions combined with a very compelling cause have brought us back together.

Our relationship with parents, in particular mothers, has an important emphasis in Buddhism. It is our mothers who bore the burden of carrying us through pregnancy, enduring the pain of giving birth to us, and taking care of us when we were vulnerable and defenceless. Although many people have to cope with childhood experiences that were less than ideal, generally speaking we are encouraged to cultivate a sense of profound gratitude towards our mothers.

We are also encouraged to think of every sentient being as if he or she had been our mother in a previous lifetime. Every purring, flying, roaring and leaping being we call not only 'sentient' but sometimes also 'mother sentient' beings in acknowledgement of this potential previous relationship.

It is a powerful, mind-altering concept. Newcomers to Buddhism may find it overwhelming. It's certainly a very different perspective from regarding pets as mere playthings: inferior, morally irrelevant and ultimately dispensable. By regarding them as mother sentient beings we are reframing the entire basis of our relationship, encouraging the cultivation of reverence, gratitude and love.

The pets with whom we share our lives have been very important to us before. We now have the opportunity to repay past kindnesses, as well as to offer them the best possible preparation for the future. In so doing we have the opportunity to create the most positive possible causes for our own future happiness. As we give, so we receive.

WE CAN DO MUCH TO HELP PETS THROUGH THE DEATH PROCESS

We live in a society squeamish and fearful about death. But avoiding this important subject does not serve us well. Buddha himself observed that focusing on one's own death is the greatest meditation. As noted earlier, there is a profound shift both in the value we attach to our life, and in what we deem to be important, when we realise just how ephemeral our existence truly is.

Contemplating death encourages us to live with greater intensity and gratitude—but this is not the only reason we do so. By acquainting ourselves with what happens when we die, and the subsequent bardo states that precede our probable next rebirth, we are better able to manage the process when it happens to us and take charge of our own destiny during this critical turning point.

We are also better able to help others who are dying.

Among the worst of times for pet lovers is when our companions become gravely ill. Our feelings of impending loss and grief are compounded by a sense of utter helplessness. Faced with a terminal diagnosis, we may believe there is nothing we can do to help our beloved pet.

In fact, there is.

Buddhism equips us with the conceptual tools to reframe what is happening, so that we focus not on ourselves and our own feelings of devastation but on how we can best help our friend, who is going through an incredibly important time of transition, their mind moving from one set of experiences, to others.

Far from being helpless, the incredibly strong karmic connection we have with our animal companion can be used to benefit them on their journey. Grief is a natural part of what we're going through, but we need to be strong for their sake, to undertake practices that are of benefit to them—and also to us.

Among the most-read blogs on my website are those concerned with how to be with your pet through the death process. This is why I am devoting a chapter in this book (Chapter Nine) to a subject that I cover in detail, given that it's something most of us have to face. We certainly don't wish for it, but dying is not only entirely natural and inevitable, many of us have it in our power to help give our pets a peaceful and positive death, setting them up for the best possible outcomes in the future. We can arguably do more for them, at this vital time, than at any other time of their lives. We are in a position of unique and great privilege and have the opportunity to act with compassion and wisdom.

BODHICHITTA IS THE MOST POWERFUL VIRTUE

Bodhichitta is the wish to become enlightened in order to lead all living beings to enlightenment. Based on compassion for the suffering we see experienced by the sentient beings all around us—not only those currently in human form—and the wish to find a permanent solution to the suffering of others as well as ourselves, bodhichitta is the most altruistic of motivations. Quite simply, no greater or more all-encompassing intention has ever been conceived.

Intention is extremely important in determining the power or weight of karma. The karmic impacts of, for example, stepping on someone's foot by accident, versus stepping on their foot to cause pain, are completely different, even though the physical action and reaction are identical. Because bodhichitta is the most benevolent of all intentions, Tibetan Buddhism suggests that the more acts of body, speech and mind motivated by bodhichitta we undertake, the more profoundly and positively our experience of reality is affected. Step by step we move towards enlightenment.

Tibetan Buddhism encourages us to recollect bodhichitta in our every action, becoming so familiar with the motivation that it becomes spontaneous and heartfelt. The process feels contrived to begin with, but it follows established psychological principles that as we think, so we become.

Pets give us multiple opportunities to recollect bodhichitta on a daily basis. In this sense, they may contribute more to our self-development than we can to theirs. Every time we feed them, cuddle them or take them for a walk, we can affirm, 'By this act of love/kindness/generosity may I achieve Buddhahood to lead all living beings to enlightenment.'

Many of the practices in this book refer to bodhichitta, the mind or heart of enlightenment, described by Shantideva in a beautiful way:

The intention to benefit all beings
Which does not arise in others even for their own sake,
Is an extraordinary jewel of the mind,
And its birth is an unprecedented wonder.

How can we help our animal companions become acquainted with this same virtue? By setting them an example of how to live. By imprinting their minds with spoken words and images affirming the goal of enlightenment. By visualising, to whatever extent we are able, our bodhichitta motivation, on the basis that the ability of animals to sense our intentions may be a lot more subtle than we generally give them credit for.

All behaviour is learned, and each one of us has the capacity to engage in enlightened actions of body, speech and mind. When we do this on behalf of our pets, they become a part of our inner journey as much as we become part of theirs. In cultivating the mind of enlightenment in relation to our animal companions, we create a virtuous spiral whose end point is of incomprehensible benefit, not only to human and pet, as we define ourselves in this lifetime, but to all sentient beings to whom we have ever felt close, reaching back for millennia to our shared primordial past, and stretching into an extraordinary, shared future of boundless and ever-increasing bliss.

CHAPTER FOUR

BEING PRESENT
FOR OUR PETS

Reiki specialist Carolyn Trethewey with Old Mate at a cat rescue centre. Carolyn advocates a mindful presence to help pets better navigate their way through traumas such as home moves, changes in the household and other stressful situations. It also promotes healing.

FOR THE PAST FIFTEEN years I have been fortunate to work from a home office. My desk overlooks a small front garden and a street that is pretty busy with office workers during the day and locals at night. Tapping away at my keyboard as the familiar, circadian rhythm repeats endlessly outside, there's one particular trend that really saddens me. Early in the morning, or late in the afternoon, when locals emerge with their dogs, instead of walking as they used to, head held high taking in the scenery, these days many people are more likely to be hunched over a mobile device, holding the dog's leash almost as an afterthought.

Sure they are going through the motions of taking the dog for a walk. But it is Dog Walk Lite. The dog is no longer the focus of their attention. Sometimes the poor animal seems to be an irritating distraction. One teenage girl, engrossed in her screen, was constantly tugging her ageing border collie's leash whenever he wanted to stop and sniff at something he no doubt found as utterly compelling as whatever had her glued to her screen.

As a society, I wonder if we are forgetting how to be present for our pets? How to honour the fact that they are conscious beings too? How, just like us, they may seek happiness, excitement and novelty. How, unlike us, much of the time their freedom of movement is constrained; for a dog, going for a walk may be his only opportunity to engage with a world that is broader than the very restricted limits of his home base.

That teenage girl I mentioned has been walking the collies since she was quite young, taking the dogs to the park being among her household responsibilities. My wife and I know her family well enough to pause on each other's doorstep for a brief chat from time to time. We know that they used to have two collies, until one died a few years ago. Last month, having not seen her out for a while, I bumped into her father who said that the remaining dog had also died.

Returning home, I felt so sorry for that dog. Sorry, especially, for the missed opportunities of his final, precious walks on earth, when he'd been denied the opportunity to pause and sniff and mark his territory, or to savour some earthy aroma, or simply to stand for a while on those four ancient legs, and take in the falling evening.

I felt sorry for the girl too. She hadn't understood how special those moments could have been. How what was evidently a daily chore could have been a final season of poignancy and grace.

Would she ever look back on those last few months of walks and wonder what she'd done?

THE BENEFITS OF QUIETER MINDS

Mindfulness is the foundation of a spiritual life. That may seem a sweeping statement. But without mindfulness, even at a superficial level, we have little capacity to take charge of our experience of reality. At a more profound level, mindfulness is required if we are to experience the true nature of our own mind, and to effect inner transformation.

What is mindfulness? Probably the most widely accepted definition of mindfulness is *paying attention to the present moment deliberately and non-judgementally.* This definition has three parts. When it comes to *paying attention to the present moment,* most of us have some awareness of what's going on at any given moment—even the girl walking the collie.

But for a lot of the time we aren't actually paying full attention to what we're seeing, hearing, smelling, tasting or touching—what neuroscientists label the 'direct' mode. Instead we're in 'narrative' mode. We're paying attention to the constant narrative flow, the cognitive chatter, the disjointed monologue going on *and on* in our head. This narrative may concern what's happened in the past, or what we wish had or hadn't happened; the future and what we hope or fear may occur. We may be caught up in analysis about the perceived failings or magnificence of ourselves or others. A survey by Harvard Psychology Department found that we spend about 47 per cent of our time in narrative mode.[1]

The *deliberate* part of the definition refers to the fact that, as humans, we need to cultivate mindfulness intentionally. We may experience mindful moments, perhaps enjoying a coffee, or admiring the moon or hugging a loved one. But we usually slip back into narrative state fairly quickly.

Being *non-judgemental* in relation to our attention to the present moment is an important element, because judgement impinges on the experience and also returns us swiftly to narrative mode: this coffee is too hot; the moon isn't as full as when I saw it last week; Veronica should have gone easier on the perfume. Blah, blah, blah ensues.

While we don't know for sure that other animals are naturally more mindful than humans, they certainly appear to be. Their vocalised communication is less complex than ours, and they rely much more heavily on non-verbal cues, including innate, intuitive perception, all of which require paying close attention to the present moment. If it is the case that animals are more mindful than humans, this places them in a stronger position to us in several very important ways.

Most immediately, consider animals' capacity for happiness. The Harvard University study found that the ability to pay attention to what is happening in the present moment is a far more accurate predictor of happiness than what we might actually be doing. A wandering mind is an unhappy mind, and mental distraction is a cause, not a consequence, of unhappiness.

Are our cats lost in mental distraction as they sit on the veranda looking out at the world? Do our dogs, sprawled out on the rug in the early afternoon, spend their time fretting about the number of hours until dinner time and what they may do to stave off boredom until then? They certainly give little evidence of this.

It's true that we humans also give little evidence of our own thoughts—which is just as well, as we may otherwise have few friends! But for proof of our own mental restlessness, all we need to do is sit down in a nice, comfortable chair in a quiet location and do absolutely nothing. Within minutes we will discover for ourselves the truth in French philosopher Blaise Pascal's famous words: 'All of human unhappiness is due to the inability to sit still in a room alone.'

GOING BEYOND THOUGHT

The recurring evidence in the early chapters of this book, that animals communicate fairly routinely in an intuitive way, both supports the notion that they are more generally mindful than we humans and offers a key insight into their potential as conscious beings.

In the West, we have traditionally regarded the development of language and intellect as going hand in hand. High level conceptual learning, thinking and creativity are considered the hallmarks of intellectual prowess. This view is shared in Buddhist traditions, but it is *not* regarded as paramount. This is because intellect, concepts and the language that supports them only take us so far.

By way of example, if you, as a chocolate lover, were approached by someone who had studied everything there is to know about chocolate, but had never actually eaten any, and if that same person offered to share his insights with you about the taste of chocolate, how much interest would you have in what he had to say? Probably very little. For all his academic learning, without any direct, first-hand experience, what could he possibly tell you, with a lifetime of chocolate-eating under your belt—perhaps quite literally?!

In exactly the same way, you can study all the many weighty tomes that have been written about the nature of consciousness and ultimate reality, and become familiar with the subtle philosophical differences between one school of thought versus another. But none of this matters compared to the direct, non-conceptual experience of your own consciousness.

When we are being mindful, we may attend to any of the senses—sight, sound, smell, taste, touch. And there is another 'sense' to which we can attend: mind. Learning to observe our own mind, instead of doing what we routinely do, which is to engage with the thoughts that arise from it, is one of the most transformative abilities we can acquire. Because it is only when we are able to let go of our constant narrative chatter, and observe the qualities of the gap between thoughts, that we are able to experience the nature of consciousness itself.

Buddhist meditators work to refine our concentration to experience the most subtle states of consciousness. We discover that mind is not a blank void, but is more like a boundless and radiant ocean from which our entire experience of reality arises. Mind also has a feeling tone, and that feeling is one of peacefulness which, with practise, deepens to the experience of profound bliss.

Verses written by revered meditation master Tilopa in the tenth century emphasise the non-conceptual nature of this form of meditation:

> Gazing intently into the empty sky, vision ceases;
> Likewise, when mind gazes into mind itself,
> The train of discursive and conceptual thought ends
> And supreme enlightenment is gained.

The mind's original nature is like space;
It pervades and embraces all things under the sun.
Be still and stay relaxed in genuine ease,
Be quiet and let sound reverberate as an echo,
Keep your mind silent and watch the ending of all worlds.[2]

As human beings living in the 21st century, being still and keeping our minds silent can seem an almost impossibly difficult challenge.

What if this comes quite naturally to animals? When I watch our cats, two elderly sisters who, at this very minute, are sitting in the dappled sunshine, staring out into the autumn morning, I have the sense that they are vividly present to what is happening, watching all that unfolds with keen interest and, when nothing in particular is happening, content simply to stay relaxed in genuine ease.

Could the simple truth about animal cognition be that they have fewer thoughts than we do, and, as a result, less mental agitation? Is it the case that their quieter, more silent minds are more attuned not only to their own consciousness, but to ours too? A greatly reduced level of mental chatter in the minds of our animal companions, far from indicating diminished spiritual capacity may, in fact, suggest the exact opposite.

What's more, a calmer state of consciousness in turn supports increased sensitivity to more subtle phenomena, making telepathy, clairvoyance and precognition a natural result. If this is the case, it would explain how animals can routinely access a more subtle mental bandwidth than many humans have ever experienced. Why they know, for example, when their owners are coming home. How they can tune in to what their human companions are perceiving in a different room. If this is true, it also underlines how fortunate we are to enjoy the affections of beings who must be incredulous about how we are able to combine such dazzling displays of mastery of our intellectual and material worlds with such shocking obliviousness to what stares us in the face.

THE OPTIMAL ENVIRONMENT FOR NURTURING OUR PETS

Given that our pets' minds are generally quieter and less agitated than our own, and that the world they experience through their senses is quite different from ours, how best do we nourish their spiritual wellbeing?

Creating an optimal environment is key.

There is no 'one size fits all' answer to suit the needs of the variety of species we may have as pets. Many parrots, for example, require relatively high levels of stimulation to stave off boredom, whereas most cats are very comfortable spending hours at a stretch in their own company. Dogs, as social beings, like to share their world with other dogs or their human counterparts. And of course not all cats, dogs or budgerigars conform to the stereotype of their species. But in every case, we need to be mindful of the fact that while our experience of reality may overlap with that of our pets, it is not the same as theirs. As a general rule, compared to us, they need peace and quiet.

Vets have long recognised that pets are stressed by loud parties and noises, including storms, fireworks and alarms; changes in the household routine, such as the presence of houseguests, or new household members—human or animal. Typical symptoms of extreme stress may see your pets hiding, trembling, defecating or urinating on a carpet or the floor, losing their appetite or becoming aggressive.

Too much noise, stimulation and emotional dramas, especially displays of aggression, take their toll on beings with quieter and more sensitive minds. What is the impact of a TV turned on first thing in the morning, and the bombardment of headlines, jingles and loud retail advertising? And that same TV left on late into the night? From an animal's perspective, it is akin to being subjected to high volume noise pollution in an incomprehensible language—and it's hardly surprising that, given the choice, many pets will choose to slip away, preferring a quiet corner somewhere else.

When we want stimulation in the form of a music fix, or a potentially raucous evening with family and friends, our pets need an escape route. If a person is hearing impaired, and needs to have the television or radio volume turned up loudly, again, what about the pets? In an environment where there is plenty of space in the home, there may be little need for concern. But in, say, a small apartment, or where only one part of a house is warm and cosy in the winter months, options like headphones may be a good way to meet both our own needs as well as those of our pets.

Being aware of pets' requirement for a peaceful, regular and nurturing environment offers the foundation for their mental well-being—and ours too.

MINDFULLY TUNING IN TO OUR PETS

Having created the right environment, how do we mindfully engage with our pets?

By paying attention to them.

Most pet lovers enjoy giving and receiving affection with pets—it's why we have them. But being mindfully present, for most of us, may require a subtle but very significant shift.

We may believe that we have a happy and caring relationship with our pet. But given the demands we face in very busy lives, the interactions we have with our pets may well be routine—that is, fairly mind-less—and heavily one-sided. We respond to a parrot's demands to be let out by going through the familiar motions of opening his cage door, letting him climb onto our arm, and perhaps offering a loving neck massage as he takes his place on the top of the cage.

At other moments, we may engage our pet in a 'conversation', perhaps getting home from work to a dog who is delighted to see us, and explaining to her how much of an outrage it is that we have to spend time this evening working on a report so that it will be delivered in time for an important deadline tomorrow. Even if the subject of our friendly patter is the dog herself—how has her day been? Has she been a good girl and resisted chewing the doormat?—what is actually happening here falls into the category of meaningless, if kindly intended, chatter. We are not really being present for our pet. We are simply using them as a proxy to give voice to our own never-ending, inner monologue.

Many of us are quite enthusiastic about talking to animals. What we're not so good at is listening to them. Being present for them. Letting go of our own endless narrative stream so that we can tune into what they may wish to tell us.

It doesn't take too much of a leap in imagination to put ourselves in the position of a being who would love to share an impression or feeling with someone, perhaps even an important message, but who finds it impossible because the other being never shuts up. We've all been there, perhaps with elderly and somewhat deaf friends and relatives. You only try so many times and then after a while, when you can't get a word in edgeways, you give up.

How amazing would it be if the other being turned round one day and said, 'I'm sorry that I spend so much time jabbering on about myself. Now I'm here for you. I'll do my best to let go of thoughts, to just be open to you and whatever you may like to communicate. I am quiet and ready right now.'

What happens when we do that? If you haven't tried it before, I suggest you try the experiment (see page 67). You may find, even in early sessions, that a shift of some kind takes place in your relationship. You open the door to a whole new dimension of possibilities when you are present for your pet.

MINDFULNESS AS THE BASIS OF COMMUNICATING WITH ANIMALS

'Long ago when animals could speak' is how folk tales of the past sometimes began, invoking the idealised innocence of a time when humans and other animals used to communicate, and shared the world in mutual appreciation, respect and balance.

'Green language' is an idea related to this, suggesting a form of communication among birds who, because of their appearance from the heavens, have traditionally been regarded as symbolising divine messengers.

Taoist writings reflect this same idea:

Even now in the country of Jie in the East, there are many people who understand the speech of domestic animals; this is a discovery possible even to our own limited knowledge. The divine sages of the most ancient times knew the habits of all the myriad things ... the fact that the sages would ... summon human beings of the eight quarters and finally assemble the birds and beasts and insects, implies that there are no great differences in mind and intelligence between living species.[3]

Living close to nature for most of our existence, humans have traditionally connected with animals in every way, from close friendships with cats and dogs that have been replayed down the ages, to awe and reverence for those animals who inspire us, and kinship with those who have spent whole lifetimes faithfully serving our needs.

But what if there *was* a time when animals could speak? Or when humans knew how to listen? Could it be that what's changed has been not so much animals' capacity to communicate as our own lost capacity to hear what they are saying?

Telepathy appears to be the basis on which many animals routinely send and receive messages, something made possible by their relatively quieter minds. As humans we have become so dislocated from nature, and our minds so agitated, that it's hardly surprising we can't hear a word that animals may be trying to tell us. Their intuitive signals come as the equivalent of a whisper from the seat beside us at a heavy metal concert.

Fortunately for us, Buddhism puts calming the mind front and centre of its practices, and provides a wealth of practical tools to help us subdue mental agitation. I share some of these in the following chapters. And it should come as no surprise that among the most practised meditation masters, subtle phenomena like clairvoyance, telepathy and precognition are considered the by-product of a more settled mind. As Buddhists we don't strive for clairvoyance. But in striving for increasingly subtle experiences of consciousness, clairvoyance quite naturally dawns.

Because Buddhism frowns on making crass displays of siddhis, or paranormal powers, the vast majority of meditators will never publicly announce that they have any special qualities, and those who do should be treated with circumspection. But if we spend time in Buddhist circles we come to discover that our actions are as apparent to our realised teachers as if they were following us via video camera. Some will even come to privately admit it is as clear as if they are watching us on TV—even when we're on the other side of the world.

In recent years the field of animal communication has grown in prominence, with an increasing number of books and training programs published by those who have come to the practice from a variety of backgrounds. Once the preserve of psychics and sooth-sayers—who, if Pope Gregory IX had had his way, would have been burned at the stake—animal communication is becoming an emerging discipline, with a growing number of practitioners, including those from traditionally left-brain backgrounds such as vets and conservationists. Some demonstrate truly amazing results in terms of helping locate lost pets, transforming the behaviour of depressed or aggressive animals, and diagnosing the cause of problem behaviours or illnesses.

What all animal communicators have in common is an ability to subdue their own minds, let go of their own thoughts, and focus instead on whatever message another being may be trying to commu-nicate. While different teachers have different points of emphasis, they tend to share a few key instructions when communicating with pets:

The importance of a peaceful environment, free from digital inter-ruption, is more conducive to subtle communication than somewhere that's noisy or where we may be disturbed.

The importance of timing, which should not coincide with a meal that is about to be served, the usual early evening walk or some other regular activity that may be a distraction.

We need to get our own minds into a relaxed and open state if we are to be receptive.

Assuming that both the animal and ourselves are relaxed and present, **we should formally ask our pet if they are willing to communicate with us.** Only if we receive a positive response should we continue, initially with a simple question.

Positive and negative responses may take a variety of forms from non-verbal action—such as your cat getting up from where they are sitting, coming over and gently head-butting you—to a thought, impression, feeling or even symbol or other image.

Responses may be delayed. We are not messaging one another on a social media platform. It may take time to get a response. We need to remain patient, focused and calm. We also need to maintain an open mind, allowing for a perhaps quite unexpected form of response.

Feel free to **experiment with imagery** such as a golden flow of light from your heart to your pet, and other visualisation which may have a significance for your pet and you.

Be willing to cultivate trust in your own intuition.

Practise!

Animal communicators universally acknowledge that while some people may possess developed skills as communicators, we are all capable of some level of communication, and many of us already communicate to some extent, although we may not always recognise it as such.

One tip I have picked up over the years is the idea that pets respond as well to imagery as they do to vocalised requests. You can call your cat to come in for the night, and depending on their mood and the warmth of the evening, they may or may not respond. But for a change, try not calling, but simply *imagine* calling, and them responding. Visualise them coming inside through the door or window. You may be surprised to find it is just as effective when, a few minutes later, your feline friend makes an appearance—or, quite possibly, doesn't!

An interesting corollary to this is to ensure that what you imagine and what you vocalise are consistent. For example, warning a pet that they must not jump on the sofa, while imagining them on the sofa, sends out mixed messages, and the visualised message may well trump the vocalised one.

The field of animal communication is intriguing and rapidly evolving, along with animal perception, cognition, pre-cognition, behaviour and relationship studies that are increasingly being undertaken around the world. For readers who are interested in exploring this subject further I recommend the work of Anna Breytenbach, which you will find at www.animalspirit.org.

EXPERIMENT: BEING MINDFULLY PRESENT FOR YOUR PET

Pick a moment when your pet is awake and alert, but not necessarily focused on an imminent meal, arrival or walk.

Sit together in a quiet place, inside or out.

Settle your mind for a minute or so by focusing on your breath. Each time you exhale, let go more and more of any thoughts and feelings.

Having settled your mind to some extent, ask your pet if they would like to share a few minutes of quality time with you. Ideally, the asking involves not only a verbalised idea, but an image of you attending to your pet, because animals can be receptive to visualised cues. During this time, assure your pet that they will remain the focus of your attention. Whatever they would like to communicate or do, you are open to them.

Wait. Watch. Don't expect the reaction to be instant. The answer may come in the form of an action—such as approaching you—a symbol, or an image. This is not text messaging.

If you get a positive response, ask your pet what he or she would most like from you.

Be open and ready to respond.

Practise regularly.

CHAPTER FIVE

FIVE BENEFITS OF PRACTISING MINDFULNESS WITH PETS

Psychologist Mel Keen with Will. Being in the presence of horses can offer emotionally safe, less threatening options for clients dealing with trauma. VICKI YEATES AT FIFTY-TWO PHOTOGRAPHY

Practising mindfulness is a deceptively gentle and simple—though not necessarily easy—process. What could be more straightforward and enjoyable than devoting quality time to our animal companion? But we shouldn't underestimate the powerful benefits of this important practice. In this chapter I explore what happens when we make a concerted effort to cultivate the regular habit of mindfulness in relation to our pets.

1.   WE DEVELOP CLOSER RELATIONSHIPS

When I put a call out to my blog readers, asking them to share examples of how practising mindfulness affected their relationships with their pets, I got a lot of messages from rueful pet lovers admitting that their pets were far more mindful of them than the other way around. Hectic lives, busy minds and cultural conditioning mean that many of us are just not in the habit of being present for our pets.

Yet we all have the capacity to change.

Salin Joseph, a technical writer from Bangalore, explained that she is a cat lover, but that work keeps her away from home for weeks at a time. During these periods, her father takes care of her cats and, as a result, she has felt the cats becoming closer to her father than to herself.

> Last time, when I went home, I decided that the time I spent with the cats I'd try to live in the present and would not think about anything else. The result was amazing. I could feel my cats connecting with me. They never used to come and sit on my lap whenever I called them. But this time it was different. I could feel the positive energy between us. In fact, they followed me when I went out of the house and they were playful and

energetic. I kept all my worries aside when my cats showed their innocent love.

I even noticed when I think about something else when I'm with them, they started going away from me. Then I realized, mindfulness is the greatest gift both for my pets and me.

When we are mindfully present for our pets, we open up the possibility of getting to know them better and become more aware of their feelings and wishes. We also deepen the relationship between us from one conducted at surface level to one that is more intuitive and heartfelt. It's possible that we sense our pet wants to communicate a message that could be expressed in words, like, 'I wish you wouldn't pick me up that way', or 'I prefer having the lights turned down'. But it's also likely that any communication could be of a non-conceptual kind—that is, not something that can be articulated so much as an impression, a feeling, a knowingness.

As described earlier in the previous chapter, conceptual thought is only one element of consciousness and, from a Buddhist perspective, not the most important one. It is the non-conceptual experience of something that matters—the taste of chocolate, rather than the theory of how chocolate tastes. The practice of driving a car, rather than the academic knowledge of how cars should be driven. The experience of being in love, rather than knowing the lyrics of a hundred love songs.

Some of us, who have learned to ignore our feelings and mistrust our intuition, find it a challenge to pay these greater heed. But they are always there, just beneath the surface. And even if we think of ourselves as entirely rational, left-brain thinkers, the truth is that we still observe and respond to the non-verbal cues of our fellow humans. Without being told, for example, we know what crossed arms or the avoidance of eye contact means in a given situation. We are still receiving non-verbal information, even if we choose not to set too much store by that particular news feed.

Being mindfully present to our pets requires us to let go of these inhibitions and allow our intuition to come into play. We will not always get it right, but there are some things we'll be unable to avoid—like the sudden eagerness of a pet to spend time with us, when we show we are willing to give them our proper attention. The feeling of closeness we have when we can communicate on a level that goes beyond words.

2. WE ARE IN A BETTER POSITION TO HELP THEM

Depending on your own personal definition of spirituality, the connection we can develop with our pets may be seen as having a spiritual dimension—it is certainly not confined to the purely material. When we're able to develop a level of mental closeness, this is a wonderfully rewarding experience in itself. From a Buddhist perspective, it also enhances our ability to help our pets to an extraordinary degree.

The extent to which we can influence any other being depends largely on our relationship with them. When our minds are closely entrained and we are able to undertake certain practices, in particular mantra recitation, the positive impact we can have on our pet's mind stream is simply incalculable. Which is why practising mindfulness in relation to our animal companion is the basis on which we can most positively propel their inner development. I outline specific practices to benefit our pets' karma in Chapter Seven.

3. THEY ARE IN A BETTER POSITION TO HELP US

Being mindfully present to our pets can offer some very practical benefits to us too. When interacting with our pets with half a mind on the phone, the TV or the social media channel, we are unlikely to notice what they may be trying very hard to tell us. Much like us attempting to break into the monologue of that hard-of-hearing elderly man standing in the shopping mall to tell him that his fly is undone. Less than subtle interruption may be required.

Pets can sometimes tell us literally life-saving things. Here is an example from Jane Johnson who lives in the Pacific Northwest, in the United States:

> My independent cat Max who is a 'I might let you pet me when I feel like it kind of cat' started sitting on my lap and wanting to knead my lower abdomen. He would follow me from room to room and keep an eye on me at all times. This went on for close to a month.
>
> I went in for a routine test about this time and found I have colorectal cancer.
>
> Max seemed aware there was something wrong before I or my doctor knew.
>
> As I have been doing chemo treatment, Max has kept an eye on me. Following me from room to room. Meows at the bathroom door until I come out. He again has his independent streak, or it is the chemicals, but he no longer sits on my lap. He rarely wants that closeness anymore.
>
> But this cat knew that I had cancer before I did.

There are a very large number of anecdotal accounts of pets and other animals trying to alert people to illnesses. A number of these accounts involve dolphins who have paid particular attention to individuals, and specific parts of their bodies, while swimming with them. In most cases, the people involved were oblivious to their own illness until tests later revealed what the dolphins seemed to be trying to tell them.[1]

Dolphins, like other cetaceans, 'see' in three dimensions, using highly sensitive sonar called echolocation. It would appear that they perceive a holographic image, similar to that produced by some medical scanning devices. That being the case, it seems no great leap to assume that they have the capacity to distinguish a diseased organ from a healthy one. Why they would wish to bring this to our attention is not a subject that has been investigated to any extent. But given the spontaneous way in which this has occurred, in some cases when people have gone swimming with wild dolphins, the simplest and most plausible explanation is empathy and goodwill.

By far the greatest number of disease identifications by animals involve dogs. While humans have relied on dogs' sense of smell—a thousand times more sensitive than our own—since our earliest days as hunter gatherers, it is only very recently that we have recognised the potentially life-saving role dogs can play in early detection of a variety of health conditions. Dogs are able to detect tiny odour concentrations of about one part per trillion—the equivalent of one teaspoon in two, full-sized Olympic swimming pools. This makes them highly sensitive to minute changes in breath and body odour.

Diabetes assistance dogs are trained to respond to scent changes that reflect dangerous shifts in blood sugar level. By communicating with their owner, in a specific way, they can provide a valuable alert so the person can take whatever action is needed—usually ingesting a fast-acting carbohydrate to avoid a hypo.

Epileptic 'seizure alert dogs' can provide the same early warning system, although the ability to predict a seizure seems to be specific to individual dogs, making training and testing more difficult. Medical Detection Dogs is a United Kingdom organisation set up to research human disease detection through canine scent. In research studies since 2002, Dr Claire Guest and her team have shown how dogs can detect certain cancers, like prostate cancer, earlier and more accurately than existing standard tests. They are currently also researching early detection of breast, lung, colorectal and other cancers as well as Parkinson's Disease.

We are only at the beginning of understanding how we can harness the vastly superior sensory abilities of other beings in ways like these. Science is increasingly able to confirm the anecdotal evidence already available—that our animal companions are not only much more sensitive to the world we share than we are, they also have the capacity to provide extremely useful feedback about our own physical wellbeing.

Other ways in which animals can help us are also becoming more widely accepted. UK charity Dogs for Good trains and provides dogs that not only help people with physical disabilities but also children with autism. Autism assistance dogs can help families do simple things like go to the shops together, which may have been impossible before. They can change an autistic child's behaviour by introducing routines, reducing bolting behaviour, interrupting repetitive actions and helping a child cope with new environments, which may otherwise seem overwhelming. Most of all, they offer an uncomplicated relationship, love and acceptance from a being whose emotions are never confusing or difficult to read.[2]

The use of therapy dogs and cats in aged care facilities is increasingly common. To some extent, we may see this merely as pets reprising a role they have had for thousands of years—providing comfort to aged humans. The only real difference is the context.

Animals are also being introduced more widely in counselling. From her premises in the hills just outside Perth, Australia, psychologist Mel Keen offers Equine Assisted Counselling and Therapy (EACT). Says Mel: 'I have observed that horses can offer an emotionally safer, less threatening option for clients to experiment with different relationship skills and re-establish closeness or intimacy with another non-human emotional being. Clients often report feeling seen and understood by a horse and this supports them to feel calm, connected and in control.'

Mel points out that the healing power of horses is far from a recent discovery. As far back as 400 BC the ancient Greeks included horse 'therapy' as part of their rehabilitation of wounded warriors. EACT is more and more widely practised in the USA and Europe as well as in Australia, and can have an especially powerful role to play in helping people deal with trauma.

'I am particularly passionate about the neurobiology of trauma, somatic processing and sensorimotor approaches to counselling and therapy,' Mel Keen explains. 'In my experience therapy horses support the process of helping clients to become aware of their bodies and patterns of behaviour. They respond to changes in human heart rates, body posture and muscle tension, so provide valuable feedback, as well as support a reduction in emotional arousal. Horses have a unique role to play in supporting psychosocial rehabilitation and working through interpersonal aspects of trauma.'

4.   WE ARE MORE TUNED IN TO THEIR EVERYDAY WISHES

If we establish a more mindful relationship with our pet, we open ourselves to a whole range of messages, including those concerning their everyday wishes. On the surface of things, these may not seem especially important but, at the time, they may be highly significant to our pet. Our own daily lives may absorb us in all kinds of activities and decisions with far-reaching consequences. Being better tuned into our pets, and making a conscious decision for moments throughout each day simply to pause, and renew that connection, can bring us back to the sometimes basic but important things we can do to help make our pets' lives happier.

Writing from Tasmania, Helen Rose says:

My episodes of communication are very small. I always know when the water bucket is getting low ... lol. This may sound strange, but I have two dogs and fill the water bucket up every morning, but with the particularly hot summer, the dogs have been drinking more water. It seems that during the day, no matter where I am, I get a 'little thought' and sure enough, I will go to the water bucket outside and it's empty.

Another sort of little communication is from my weimaraner, Wilson, I seem to be closer to him than our doberman. When they have been walked, I let Wilson have a little sleep on our bed. I close the door so that Sam the doberman can't annoy him and he has a little rest and sleep. I can go into the bedroom numerous times and he is asleep. I will be doing housework or just stuff, and the thought will come to me: 'I want to come out now.' And sure enough, I will go to the bedroom door and there Wilson is, just waiting for me to open the door for him. He never barks or whines, but I just know when he wants out.

Horse owners have written in with very similar stories. In one case, a woman visited her retired horse in his field only every few days. But one day she was struck very suddenly and strongly by the urgent need to visit. When she did, she found he had become lame.

She said she sensed his relief as she arrived, knowing that he would soon be taken care of.

Many readers will be able to relate to these 'everyday' examples of being tuned in to our pets. We may glance up from the sofa and see the face of our dog at the window, wanting to be let in. Sometimes in the afternoon, I will be working at the computer when Kahlua, our tortoiseshell cat, will stroll across my office in the direction of the meditation cushion and sit down beside it, a pointed reminder that it's time for the afternoon session—Kahlua loves to sit next to me when I meditate.

A more mindful relationship with our pet enables us to be more aware and responsive to their needs on an everyday basis.

5. WE CAN RESPOND MORE EFFECTIVELY IN TIMES OF CRISIS

A mindful connection also enables us to act more effectively in times of crisis by opening a channel of communication that wouldn't otherwise be available.

Noelene Bolton from Sydney shares her story:

I had a friend transporting a golden retriever for me from Canberra to Sydney, and when they stopped at Sutton Forest for a break they decided to let her have a walk. Unfortunately she got free and bolted into the bush. They arrived home at night devastated because they couldn't find her, but we worked out a plan to go and look for her the next day. As I was going to bed I just got this message in my head 'Go to Sutton Forest, she is waiting for you.' I got changed, got into my car, and drove to Sutton Forest—over an hour's drive. When I arrived there I thought what do I do now? I turned off the highway, went down a road, decided to do a U-turn—and my car headlights shone on her behind a fence. I always follow my instinct even if I don't know why, and this time it sure paid off.

Recognising that animals communicate telepathically, and being willing to act on the messages we receive—even if it involves driving for an hour in the middle of the night—can empower us to help our pets, especially in times of crisis. Paying attention to such messages, especially in our pet's greatest hour of need, is a recurring experience of pet lovers.

Mindfulness supports this process by improving our ability to let go of the constant thoughts that fill our minds, enhancing our sensitivity to receiving messages and making us more confident about acting on an ancient and innate method of communication.

FIVE TIPS FOR PRACTISING MINDFULNESS WITH PETS ON A DAILY BASIS

1. Acknowledge your pets every morning when you awake. Even if you may be half asleep and grumpy because it's a week day and you need to go to work, remember that a pet's life is short. Each new day is one of a precious few compared to what humans can expect. Try to acknowledge to your animal companion, the gratitude you feel having them in your life. And be open to how they are feeling, here and now.

2. Set aside at least two ten-minute sessions each day as dedicated pet time, to spend stroking the tummies, scratching the necks or otherwise enjoying the company of whatever

animals you share your life with. Take this time to let go of your thoughts and tune into how your pet is feeling. Make yourself available to the impressions, feelings and messages they may wish to share with you.

3.   When arriving home, as you and your pet see each other, take a few moments to acknowledge them by name, let go of whatever you were thinking about and give them your full attention. Reaching down to give them a pat while talking on your phone is not a greeting. Also, how you are feeling is only half the story. How is your pet feeling, right now?

4.   When you take your dog for a walk, leave the phone at home, or at least resolve to keep it in your pocket and use it only for an urgent or important call.

5.   Last thing at night, when you switch the light off, reach out to your pets physically—if you share a bed—or, if they are elsewhere in the house, in your mind, and remind them how much they mean to you, and the special place they have in your life and heart. Be open to whatever they may wish to communicate.

CHAPTER SIX

MEDITATING WITH OUR PETS

David meditating with Kahlua. In the afternoons, if she feels I have been at my desk too long, Kahlua will walk directly across my keyboard and jump down on the carpet, reminding me to stick to my priorities. JANMARIE MICHIE

IF MINDFULNESS IS PAYING attention to the present moment deliberately and non-judgementally, what is meditation? One definition of meditation is the application of mindfulness to a particular object for a specific period of time. For example, we may choose to be mindful of some element of breathing—say, the sensation at the tip of our nostrils as we inhale and exhale, as we count our breaths in cycles of four. And we may decide to do this for ten minutes.

We're now meditating.

Buddhism has a somewhat different definition of meditation: thoroughly familiarising the mind with a virtuous object. This is because Buddhism directs meditation to our ultimate enlightenment.

Whether we practise meditation for spiritual or purely secular benefits, it's fair to say that meditation, or mind training, is to a mindful life what physical training is to a physically fit life. The one practice supports the other. If you work out at the gym regularly, you're going to be able to carry heavy luggage, ascend flights of stairs, and deal with whatever physical challenges you encounter each day with much greater ease than a sedentary person. In just the same way, practising meditation regularly enables you to deal with stressful work demands, aggressive people and whatever mental challenges you encounter with greater ease than a person who has fewer mental resources.

A myriad benefits of meditation have already been established in scientific trials, showing how we benefit physically and psychologically from the practice. And much more research is currently underway. If you're interested in exploring these fascinating subjects in detail, you may like to read my book *Why Mindfulness Is Better Than Chocolate*.

CAN ANIMALS REALLY MEDITATE?

It is often said that dogs, cats and other animals are natural meditators. They are capable of sitting still for great lengths of time, gazing into the mid-distance and appearing simply to abide in the moment without the need for physical movement or mental stimulation. Unlike us, they seem capable of sitting in a quiet room alone.

Whether or not they are *meditating*, according to the definitions outlined above, is as unknowable as whether or not the person sitting next to us on the meditation cushion is meditating, or simply daydreaming. But the way that so many pets are highly sensitive to all forms of non-verbal communication as well as quite naturally intuitive and even telepathic suggests that, at the very least, they spend long periods abiding in the here and now—being present.

In the wisdom traditions of the East, the role of meditation has had a particular focus: it is the means by which we can understand and experience the nature of our own consciousness. The great advantage of meditation is that it enables a direct, non-conceptual experience of our own mind—something of greater personal value to us than a purely theoretical understanding.

There is no reason why our pets may not also have this same experiential-based understanding of consciousness. Reading books, listening to teachings and developing a conceptual framework may be helpful to those of us who are obsessive compulsive thinkers. But at some point we need to learn to let go of thoughts and simply observe consciousness for what it is. In this particular activity, our pet dog or cat may be a more advanced practitioner than we are!

A FEW TIPS ON MEDITATING WITH PETS

I expect that many readers of this book will already have some experience of meditation. If you are new to the practice, or would like a quick refresher, I have provided a 'How to meditate' section, providing essential instructions, later in this chapter. You can also access free downloads of a variety of guided meditations on my website: www.davidmichie.com.

When meditating with pets, do you need to change how you go about your practice? If your meditation is in some way pet-focused, for example in the case of healing (see Chapter Eight), then the content of your session will necessarily be different. Generally, the only other way I suggest you change your meditation routine is with the following practical steps.

ENABLE YOUR PETS TO COME AND GO FROM WHERE YOU ARE MEDITATING

When my wife and I were first adopted by our cat, Princess Wussik— the inspiration behind *The Dalai Lama's Cat* series—I continued my practice of shutting my office door every morning to meditate in peace and quiet. After a few days of this, there was a scratching at the door. I ignored it, in the way that meditators train to withdraw attention from external noises.

The scratching became more insistent. As did my efforts to ignore it.

When, after a break, the scratching started again, I gave in to the inevitable. I got up, opened the door and let little Wussik come over to where I was sitting, where she settled beside me and began to purr appreciatively. It was still a noise, but one I could happily adjust to.

Wussik is no longer with us, and since that time my wife and I have shared our lives with other cats. I no longer close the door when

I meditate, but use a door stop to keep it open just wide enough for a small, furry body to pass through.

For the sake of your own meditative concentration, as well as your pet's convenience, I suggest you keep a door or window open, to allow your pet to come or go during the course of the session without disturbing you.

These days I often find that as I end my meditation session, but before I am ready to get up, my current meditation buddy Kahlua will roll over next to me, with a tremulous stretch of arms and legs, before getting up and walking out of the room. It's as though she's saying 'That's the meditation done. What next?'

LET YOUR PET DECIDE ON PHYSICAL CONTACT

I know that some people suggest you should meditate with your hand placed on your dog, rabbit, pig or cat to provide contact and reassurance. My own view is that there is a reason why the seven point meditation posture has been used by meditators for the past 2500 years, and that's why I keep my hands, like a pair of shells, in my lap, even if a pet is right beside me.

Your pet doesn't need you to touch them to benefit from your peacefulness of body and mind when you meditate. Your pet senses this, even if they are at the other end of the house. Because they are more intuitively engaged with us than most of us generally experience, they are well aware when you shift into the unique state created by meditation—that is, a relaxed body combined with a focused mind.

Of course, if your pet decides they want to lie right beside you, or even climb onto your lap, it's up to you how far you accommodate them without detracting from your session. I was amused by the description Judy Sampson-Hobson shared in an email about her large tabby cat Charlie, who loved to hug, nuzzle and purr loudly.

When you found yourself meditating, Charlie was there. However, he was much more Zen about his contact. He would very slowly and quietly make his way onto your lap, even if it meant crawling under a shawl. Curl into a generous yet stealthy 13 lb ball, and purr much more quietly, so as not to disturb, and fall fast asleep.

This description exactly mirrors how I have heard dog lovers describe the not-so-surreptitious attempts by large canine friends to sneak onto their laps when they are trying to meditate!

OUT OF SIGHT IS NOT OUT OF MIND

You can no more force a pet to meditate than you can a human. Eager as you may be to have your pet accompany you when you meditate, it is better to extend an open invitation, rather than make any demands. And you certainly shouldn't try to shut a reluctant guinea pig or rabbit in the room when you are meditating in the hope that they will be caught up in the wonderful energy you are creating.

Although we may have mostly lost the ability to tune into the minds of others, there is much evidence that our pets have not. As far as they are concerned, just because we are out of sight doesn't put us out of range. They may be very aware of what we're doing on the meditation cushion but, for whatever reason, feel disinclined to join us. They may prefer to share the experience with us in mind rather than in body. Or not even that. It is their prerogative.

Even if our pet isn't physically present when we meditate, this doesn't mean they don't appreciate or benefit from what we're doing. If we're new to the practice, it may take them a while to warm up to it. Don't make your own meditation journey contingent on your pet being with you. It is enough that you cultivate our own sense of wellbeing, balance and clarity of mind. They will be among the first beneficiaries.

THE BENEFITS OF MEDITATING WITH OUR PETS

OUR PETS BECOME CALMER

Pets entrain their minds with ours and are highly responsive to our own emotional state. Think how easy it is to get a dog excited by jumping up and down and shouting enthusiastically. Within a few seconds, most dog owners can have their pet dog barking and jumping too, through the effect sometimes known as emotional contagion.

Pets also respond when we become calmer and more relaxed. And of all the proven benefits of meditation, the multiple outcomes of the relaxation response, physical as well as psychological, are probably the most well established. Meditation has been proven to boost our immune defences, help us manage pain, act as an anti-inflammatory, counteract anxiety and depression, and enhance our sense of wellbeing, to list only a few advantages. When we meditate, even as beginners, we start to tap into the profound peacefulness and wellbeing of our own primordial mind.

If we meditate with our pets we open the possibility for them to experience these same benefits. Research has yet to establish the extent of impacts, but anecdotal evidence of the very strong way that pets are attracted to us when we meditate suggests that they are powerfully drawn to the psycho-physical shift we create, perhaps because they are able to respond to this same shift themselves, or because they are attracted by our transition to a state of greater coherence, which reinforces their own capacity for wellbeing.

WE BUILD STRONGER BONDS OF TRUST

Engaging regularly in a shared activity, especially a non-conceptual one, quite naturally strengthens bonds between those who participate. As I tell the corporate groups to whom I teach mindfulness, 'A company that sits together, knits together.' There is a sense that we share something that is distinct from other activities ('set apart' is, in fact, the original meaning of the word 'sacred'), something important and beneficial that binds us together. This very much applies when we meditate with our pets. The longer we continue our meditation journey together, the stronger the bonds.

WE ENHANCE THE TRAINING PROCESS

A direct consequence of stronger bonds is an increased willingness to do other things for one another. We know each other and, in the most important sense, feel we are essentially on the same page. It is unsurprising that dog trainers report that meditating with pets enhances the training process, given the foundation of trust that has been established.[1]

WE CAN SHIFT THE DYNAMICS IN A DIFFICULT RELATIONSHIP

Meditation offers a different way to be together, quite separate from our usual vocalised or visualised modalities. Our pets come to experience a different side to us, one which they can more readily share. Sometimes this can be all that's needed to remove quite significant obstacles from a difficult relationship.

I have received a number of emails from people reporting how a pet that was withdrawn or aloof, often after having been rescued from the local animal shelter, changed their behaviour when they encountered their person meditating.

I particularly like this story from a reader in the United States:

> When I first met my partner Peter, my tabby cat Marney did not particularly like him. She seemed to take delight in sitting on his lap, letting him fuss her, then scratching and biting him.

Nothing new there—I hear people saying that most cats do not like change, but as Peter is allergic, he could have had a nasty reaction very quickly. This led to our evenings together being cut short as Peter had to go home to get away from the 'catness'.

To give him credit, Peter persevered with us. He started taking antihistamines regularly and about ten months later he moved in with me. Marney was still indifferent to him with no love lost between them. If Peter felt 'catty' he would retreat to the spare bedroom, which was kept a cat-free zone.

Peter started to meditate using the technique of mindfulness of the breath and did this in the privacy of the spare bedroom with the door shut. One evening he did not shut the door properly and Marney wandered in. She jumped on the bed and lay down with Peter as he meditated. He didn't shoo her away and just left her alone and she stayed with him, seeming to relax and enjoy the atmosphere, rolling on her back and being completely at ease with him for the first time since they met. She often joins him now, relishing the peace, and even seems to know when he is going to meditate and not just going upstairs. She's much more affectionate towards him and has not bitten or scratched since, which leads to some lovely evenings, all three of us curled up on the sofa, one happy family.

The simple and gentle practice of meditation offers a potential circuit-breaker in challenging relationships like the one between Marney and Peter. It is astonishing how powerfully the dynamics can be shifted to a place of acceptance and even warmth, without the need for any other intervention, or even for a word to be said.

I can vouch for the ability of pets to tell the difference between when we're meditating versus when we're just sitting in a chair. On occasion, while still in my desk chair, I have decided to spend a few minutes reciting mantras. Within moments, Kahlua has appeared, eager to sit on the desk next to me. On other occasions, I've started meditating when she's been fast asleep on the porch outside. Awakening some way through the session, she will typically appear with a high-pitched meow that seems to me to express dismay at missing out.

WE CAN HELP OUR PETS THROUGH TIMES OF TRANSITION

Going through a rescue centre, being rehomed with a new family, or moving houses with the same family . . . these upheavals can cause pets a huge amount of stress. Losing loved ones—human or animal—or having to accommodate new household members, are also times of major transition where meditating with pets can play a key role in minimising trauma.

Not so long ago, a couple we knew brought home two six-year-old dachshund sisters from the local Dogs' Refuge Home. Having never formally adopted pets before, they weren't sure how they would settle. At the Dogs' Refuge Home they were told not to overwhelm their new dogs with too much excitement, to establish a routine from day one, and to allow the dachshunds plenty of time to get used to their new environment.

On arriving home, after initial exploratory visits throughout the house, the dogs seemed to adjust to their new setting very quickly. The very next day, when family members descended for a barbecue, they welcomed them with wagging tails as though they knew them of old.

Every pet is different, as is the relationship with their people. And meditation has a big impact on that relationship. On day one, when the dogs' new owners sat down to meditate for the first time since the adoption, both dogs came into the room of their own accord and sat with them. Over time one dog has developed a preference for meditating with the wife, and the other prefers being with the husband. So eager are they to maintain the habit that they are often waiting by the meditation room door for one or both of their owners to appear for the morning session.

Within weeks of being adopted, it was as though the two dachshies had been with the couple for years. The dogs were to reveal very different personalities, and came to negotiate favourite spots inside and out. Visitors would remark how very settled they seemed—as though the dogs and their new owners had been living together for their whole lives.

While the impact of meditation on this particular transition can't be proven, the owners have no doubt that the sisters benefited from the calming effect of being in a home with two meditators, and that this helped them feel safe and settled.

Providing time each day for both ourselves and our pets to reconnect with the peace and light within helps us cope when our world is turned upside down. As we come to terms with whatever has changed in conventional reality, it is extremely beneficial to experience, on a daily basis, the more enduring reality that, ultimately, all is well.

WE BECOME MORE MINDFUL OF OUR PETS DURING THE DAY

It is sometimes observed that mindfulness is easy to do—it is *remembering to do it* that is the hard part. While it's possible to cultivate mindfulness purely through incidental activity—for example, remembering to be mindful whenever we enjoy a meal, or take a shower—we experience higher levels of mindfulness if we begin each day with a meditation session. Meditation is the best way to turbo-charge our practice of mindfulness.

When we meditate with our pets, we strengthen the habit of being mindful of them. Developing a closer relationship and sharing the same mindfulness experience, the off-cushion time we spend together is more likely to be mindful. We also make ourselves more accessible to them and optimise the potential for non-verbal communication to occur.

WE OPEN THE PATHWAY TO HEALING

Meditation and healing are very closely related. Many reiki practitioners would say that meditation *is* healing. The habit of meditating with our pets opens the door to our ability to focus beneficial attention and energy on their physical wellbeing, a subject explored in greater detail in Chapter Eight. Because pets entrain their minds so much with our own mental state, when we place ourselves in a state of balance, congruence and wellbeing, the same shift occurs for them too. With an understanding of specific methods to help the wellbeing of others, we can support their physical and psychological recovery in a gentle yet very powerful way.

WE CREATE TRANSFORMATIONAL IMPRINTS

While the benefits listed above are all valid, from a Buddhist perspective the main purpose of meditation is not to manage stress or enhance relationships. These are only beneficial side effects. The real purpose of meditation is to enable inner growth in a way that is only possible by experiencing the true nature of our own mind directly and non-conceptually.

When we meditate with our pets, quite apart from whatever immediate benefits may be derived, we are also imprinting their consciousness, or conditioning them, so that they will be predisposed to meditate in future lives. We are helping them familiarise their minds with an object of virtue. If they come to associate the state of meditation with peace and positivity, we have given our pets the most wonderful karmic inheritance. What's more, if they become familiar with the sound of a transformational mantra, the Buddhist view is that this alone may be the cause for them to experience higher rebirth in their next life.

In summary, when we meditate with our pets, we benefit them not only in the short term. We can make the most profound and positive impact on their minds, empowering their own journey to enlightenment.

HOW TO MEDITATE: INSTRUCTIONS

WHERE AND WHEN?

A quiet room, first thing in the morning, is recommended for meditation. It suits most people because after a good night's sleep we tend to be more refreshed, and our minds less cluttered, than in the evening.

FOR HOW LONG?

I would suggest you start with ten or fifteen minutes if you're new to the practice. It's important that meditation is not a chore for you but something you want to do, at the very least a matter of curiosity, and hopefully developing into the source of greatly enhanced inner peace. Ideally you will end a session feeling positively about what you've just done, instead of relieved it's all over. By starting with bite-sized chunks, you will want to increase the length of your sessions quite naturally as your concentration improves. While some meditators put a watch in front of them to keep track of time, if you find this creates a distraction you may like to use a gentle alert on your mobile.

PHYSICAL POSTURE

Take off your shoes and loosen any tight clothing such as a belt. Ideal meditation clothing is a T-shirt or sweatshirt, shorts or tracksuit pants, or a dressing-gown.

Sit with a straight back. Sitting cross-legged on a cushion on the floor has been the recommended posture for thousands of years. But if you can't manage this, because of a bad back, sore knees or for some other reason, it's fine to sit in a straight-backed chair. Of all the posture instructions, this is the most important because your spine is the main conduit of your central nervous system. Your back should be erect, but following its natural tendency to be slightly curved at the base. When you meditate, it's important to keep the spine neither slumped nor artificially straight. This instruction holds true whether you are sitting on a meditation cushion or a regular chair, or even lying in bed.

Rest your hands in your lap. Place your right hand in the left, palms upwards like a pair of shells, with your thumb tips meeting approximately at the level of your navel.

Relax your shoulders. Ideally they should be slightly rolled back, down and resting level. Your arms will therefore rest loosely by your sides.

Adjust the tilt of your head. If you are feeling particularly agitated, tilt your head slightly down, as that will help reduce the agitation. If you're feeling drowsy, keep your head more upright, to help get rid of sleepiness.

Relax your face. Your mouth, jaw and tongue should be neither slack nor tight, and your brow should be smooth. By placing the tip of the tongue behind your front teeth, you can help control the build-up of saliva.

Close your eyes or gaze at a spot a metre or two ahead of you in an unfocused way. While keeping your eyes half-open and gazing downwards is recommended, when beginning to meditate most people find that keeping the eyes fully closed is better for eliminating distraction.

PSYCHOLOGICAL POSTURE

Once you are in the optimal physical posture, take a few deep breaths and, each time you exhale, **let go of whatever thoughts, feelings and sensations you may have been experiencing.** Use this exercise as a punctuation mark between whatever was going on before in your mind, and the meditation session you are about to begin. As far as possible try to be purely in the present, without a past, without a future, simply abiding in the here and now.

Give yourself permission to meditate. For the next period of time it's okay not to have to think about any of your usual concerns. This is your time off to restore, recharge and rebalance.

Begin with a clear motivation. I have provided two options below, one for newcomers to meditation and Buddhism, and the other for people who have some level of commitment to Tibetan Buddhism.

SECULAR MOTIVATION
By the practice of this meditation
I am becoming calm and relaxed,
Happier and more efficient in all that I do,
Both for my own sake, as well as for others.

Feel free to personalise this to reflect your own priorities. Remember that statements should be written in the present tense, not the future, and should be stated in the positive (e.g. I am becoming more and more patient) not the negative (e.g. I am becoming less and less angry). You should also include the wellbeing of others in your motivation.

TIBETAN BUDDHIST MOTIVATION

This combines the three practices of taking refuge (in the Buddha, Dharma and Sangha), a commitment to practise the six perfections (generosity, ethics, patience, joyous perseverance, concentration and wisdom), and establishing the mind of bodhichitta:

> To the Buddha, Dharma and Sangha
> I go for refuge until becoming enlightened.
> By the practice of giving and so on,
> May I achieve Buddhahood to benefit all beings.

It's useful to learn a motivation off by heart so you can repeat it three times, eyes closed, at the start of a session. In this way you associate a relaxed physical and psychological state with this verse.

MEDITATION 1: BREATH COUNTING

Breath counting is used widely across most meditative traditions, and through all levels, from novice meditators to the most advanced practitioners. There are a number of reasons for this. The breath is a convenient object of meditation because we have no difficulty finding it. Making it the focus of our attention is an entirely natural process. When we do so, our breathing tends to slow down quite naturally, thereby slowing our entire metabolism and making us feel more relaxed. And achieving a calm but focused state serves as a useful stabilisation practice.

With the following breath-counting exercise, the objective is to actively shift our focus to the breath. We do this, quite simply, by mentally counting each breath on exhalation, for a set number of breaths. I recommend from one to four to begin with, before beginning again at one.

The process is as follows: place the focus of your attention at the tip of your nostrils, like a sentry, and observe the flow of air as you breathe in and then out. Ideally all the air you inhale and exhale should be through your nose, with your mouth kept firmly shut. However, if you have a condition that makes this difficult, by all means part your lips slightly to inhale and exhale.

As you breathe out, count the number 'one' in your mind, then on the next out-breath 'two', then 'three', 'four', and so on. Don't focus on anything else—for example, don't follow the air travelling into your lungs, or your rib cage rising and falling. Don't allow your mind to wander from the tip of your nostrils. And try not to fall asleep!

What we're setting out to achieve is really very simple—but not necessarily easy. The best way to discover this for yourself is to try it. Pretty soon, you'll find all kinds of thoughts demanding your attention. Even though you've set this time aside for meditating, habitual agitation or drowsiness may very soon kick in, to the point that you may discover you can't even count to four!

This is called gross agitation and it happens to us all. When it does, once you realise you've lost the object of meditation—the breath—simply refocus on it and start back at one again. Try not to beat yourself up about your lapse of attention or fall into the trap of believing that you're one of the few people who can't meditate. Your experience is, in fact, totally normal. Our minds are amazingly inventive at coming up with reasons to avoid self-discipline: you shouldn't buy into any of them!

As you settle into your practice, your focus on the breath will become sharper. Try paying more concentrated attention to the detail of every moment. The subtle, physical sensation at the tip of your nostrils as you breathe in. The coolness of the air. The warmer sensation as you exhale. Notice the start of each in-breath, how it builds up, then how it tapers off. The gap between in- and out-breaths. Then the start, middle and fading away of each exhalation. The much longer gap at the end of each exhalation.

As you progress into a meditation session, your breathing will probably slow, and you'll become more and more conscious of the gaps between out-breath and in-breath. What do you focus on then? Only the absence of breath and the complete relaxation you experience with nothing to distract you, and no demands being put on you. This may not seem an ambitious goal but, rest assured, it is profoundly calming.

Breath-based meditations are a rapid and powerful way of shifting your psycho–physical state. Within minutes you should feel calmer and more grounded. Given the established capacity of animals in general, and our pets in particular, to respond intuitively to us, when we cultivate a state of profound peace and wellbeing within ourselves, they are also prime beneficiaries. I experience the simple truth of this every day when my cat behaves as though magnetically attracted to me when I start to meditate. She will often come and curl up right next to me and begin to purr—quite unlike other times of the day when she sometimes treats me as though I have a highly contagious disease!

The subjective experiences of physical and mental wellbeing are reason enough to practise meditation. But there are other, less immediately evident but very powerful benefits outlined in this chapter, and in the one that follows.

GIVE YOUR MEDITATION A FORMAL ENDING

Just as you began with a motivation, it is useful to end with one too. Why bother? Because your mind–body state has shifted, repeating the same words now may have greater impact, like the stone thrown into a tranquil lake.

SECULAR ENDING
By the practice of this meditation
I am becoming calm and relaxed,
Happier and more efficient in all that I do,
Both for my own sake, as well as for others.

TIBETAN BUDDHIST ENDING
To the Buddha, Dharma and Sangha
I go for refuge until becoming enlightened.
By the practice of giving and so on,
May I achieve Buddhahood to benefit all beings.

MEDITATION 2: COCOON VISUALISATION

Follow the instructions above for adopting the optimal physical and psychological posture.

Visualise yourself sitting at the centre of a great cocoon of golden light. The gold light represents radiant happiness, boundless energy and abundant fulfilment in health, prosperity, relationships and all things. With your next inhalation, imagine you are breathing in this golden light and all its wonderful qualities. Visualise the light streaming into your body. With each breath you are filled with more and more happiness, more energy and more fulfilment. If you are meditating with your pet, feel free to include your pet in the visualisation, with the light flowing into their body too.

Make this visualisation relevant to where you are right now. If there is an aspect of your own or your pet's physical or emotional wellbeing that has been concerning you, imagine the golden light dissolves away all negativities, anxieties or fears. For the next few minutes, breath by breath, every aspect of your own and your pet's life is filled with positive energy, confidence and profound wellbeing.

Continuing the meditation, visualise the gold-coloured light permeating your whole body, from the crown of your head to the tips of your toes. Imagine it penetrating every part of your body, every organ—and that of your pet—each single cell, infusing your whole being with intense radiance, happiness and fulfilment. With every breath, you absorb the qualities of profound wellbeing more and more, until you become one with the golden-coloured light. You and your pet *become* energy and purpose and deep, deep happiness.

Coming to the end of your guided visualisation, be aware of how you are feeling. Enjoy the positive effect of your meditation on body and mind. Resolve to return to this feeling, as much as possible, during the rest of the day or evening.

End the meditation session by repeating your motivation.

A lot of people enjoy the novelty and playfulness of this visualisation, as well as its powerful impact on our state of body and mind. Feel free to customise the visualisation to meet your own particular needs by changing the colour of the light you breathe in. For example, deep blue is the colour of healing and this can be a most useful meditation to support physical and mental recovery from disease and illness. Bear in mind that cats and dogs can only see yellow/gold and blue, so these are the best colours to work with when meditating with pets.

These two meditations are useful to begin with, but there are many others. 'Meditation' is a bit like the word 'sport', encompassing a great many different practices, some of which appeal to different people more than others. What's important is to find the practice that most resonates with you and cultivate it.

You will find more meditation types in Chapter Eight (on healing). I also have a range of free guided meditation downloads available on my website: www.davidmichie.com.

CHAPTER SEVEN

KARMA: GUIDING OUR PETS TO A MORE POSITIVE FUTURE

The magnificent Yeshe is fortunate to be surrounded by
Buddhist imagery and loves meditating with his person, author
Debra Denker. DEBRA DENKER

WHATEVER SPECIES WE CURRENTLY belong to, our present experience of reality isn't something that has happened by chance. It is the result of previously created causes. This is the view of Buddhism.

Within the context of a single lifetime, it is also the perspective of many psychologists, who point to the way that our world view is shaped both in the formative years of childhood—not to mention puppyhood and kittenhood—as well as by a constantly shifting kaleidoscope of influences, outer and inner.

Of these, inner influences are considered the more important because, while we may not be able to control external events, we can learn to manage our own mind. In so doing, we gain control of our experience of reality. As Buddha said in *The Dhammapada*, a collection of his teachings written in verse form:

Mind is the forerunner of all actions.
All deeds are led by mind, created by mind.
If one speaks or acts with a serene mind, happiness follows,
As surely as one's shadow.

The idea that things need to be a certain way for us to be happy is, from a Buddhist perspective, an unfortunate superstition. But our consumerist culture, where advertisers set out to define specific problems which their products can fix, continually reinforces this false premise. If we have any doubt at all that that sleek German luxury car, or a house in a particular suburb, or a partner who is more like our favourite movie star isn't a true cause of happiness, all we need to do is make an assessment of people who already live with these things and people.

As far as we're able to gather, are they happier than people who don't enjoy their circumstances or relationships? Taking in the whole package—that is, the obligations of their lifestyle as well as the pay-offs—are they really to be envied?

It so happens that the suburbs of the city in which I live where antidepressants are most heavily prescribed also happen to be the wealthiest postal codes. I am sure Perth, Australia, is quite typical in that regard.

Money can provide financial solutions, but it can't deliver a sense of meaning, self-acceptance, equanimity, love or heartfelt connection to others, to name just a few of the qualities from which happiness arises as a delightful by-product.

Buddhism encourages us to cultivate these qualities of mind if we wish to experience profound wellbeing both now and in the future. If we wish for happiness, we should create the causes of happiness. If we wish to avoid suffering, we should avoid creating the causes of suffering. On a conventional level, this explanation is pretty straightforward, even if our own personal conditioning doesn't always make it easy for us to be as open-hearted or even-tempered as we would like.

How do we help others cultivate these happiness-creating qualities? Whether those others are humans or pets, there are limits on the extent to which we can shift their inner lives. But we do have some influence, even if we're not always aware of it.

This chapter explores what some of the most important influences are, and offers practical suggestions on how to use them. Our objective in familiarising our pets with specific states, sounds and imagery is not only to encourage a positive experience of reality for them in this particular lifetime. Our purpose is far more panoramic.

POSITIVE CAUSES DELIVER POSITIVE EFFECTS

The Buddhist view is that causality, or karma, is not confined to this particular lifetime, but extends well into the future. This raises the stakes considerably. Every action of body, speech and mind creates an imprint that will change the way we experience reality, but its full impact may not be felt until a future lifetime.

If you want to know what kind of life you had in a previous lifetime, Buddhists say, look at your experience in this one. If you want to know what kind of life you will have in the future, ask yourself what causes you are creating: is your life entirely self-focused, or is there space in your heart and mind for the wellbeing of others? Do you enjoy being generous? And exercise patience? How much ethical restraint do you practise when tempted by something, or someone, even when you know that acting on your drives or wishes will hurt others?

The cause of a human life is said to be virtue. So, dear reader, you know you have been virtuous in the past, even if you have been up to mischief in this one! Generosity is the cause of wealth, and patience of being attractive, to give a few of the more materially relevant examples of causality. Importantly, the karma that propels our mind stream is not inert and stable, but dynamic and multiplying, so that even quite modest causes can, when they meet with certain conditions, result in consequences way beyond the original action. Intention is a key factor in giving karma its weight.

Of particular interest to pet lovers is the way that karma propels us into a particular experience as human or animal. As my teacher, the highly regarded lama Geshe Acharya Thubten Loden, explains in his book, *Path to Enlightenment in Tibetan Buddhism*: 'Throwing karma is so called because it "throws" a rebirth. Completing karma determines the circumstances of the life you are "thrown" into.'[1]

Positive throwing karma may propel you into a human rebirth, but negative finishing karma may have you experiencing sickness, poverty and war. Geshe-la also provides the following example: 'A rebirth state thrown by negative karma and completed by positive karma, such as rebirth in the animal realm, but as a corgi belonging to the Queen.'[2]

A human rebirth is considered the best of all possible outcomes, because as humans we are able to identify and cultivate those specific practices that will lead to a better future and ultimately our enlightenment. This is not to say that animals cannot create the virtue required to help achieve future transcendence. Only that our capacity to do so is very much greater.

I am sometimes sent messages by readers saying they consider animals to be morally superior to humans, given that they don't engage in the wanton, systematic abuse of their own kind or others, that they aren't rapaciously destroying our shared environment at a terrifying speed, and for various other reasons. Collectively, the human track record is certainly patchy. But on an individual basis, as human beings, our capacity to help ourselves as well as others is generally much greater than even the most well-intentioned dolphin.

What really matters is the degree to which we use this precious and finite opportunity.

THE GREATEST PURPOSE EVER CONCEIVED

'What's the point?' I am sometimes asked, after describing the Buddhist perspective that all beings are born, live, grow old and die, only to repeat the same process, *ad infinitum*, propelled by the karma we have created. We have all been kings and slaves, animal and human, saints and villains. Round and round the cycle we go, mostly unaware of the dynamics at work, the game that's being played.

'What's the point?' is a very good question. And whether we ask it of our current life, or of the broader context, the answer is always the same: there is no point, unless we choose to create one. The start of our personal path to enlightenment begins when we have had enough of the endless suffering of samsara—a mind propelled by karma and delusion—and make the decision to break free of it.

One of the best known symbols of Buddhism is the lotus, which symbolises this journey. Rooted in the mud that represents cyclic existence, the lotus rises above everything in its swampy environment, to blossom at the surface in flowers of the most transcendent beauty.

No mud, no lotus.

Any objective overview of life on planet earth today would find it hard to avoid the self-evident suffering, whether warfare or poverty, and the relentless, dysfunctional busyness we find in the human realm, or the countless millions born into factory farming, and 3000 killed in abattoirs *every second* of the animal realm. And these are just a few top-of-mind examples.

While there is no quick fix, there is a way out of all this, on paths that have been trodden by millions before us. We owe it to ourselves, as well as to those we care about, to be aware of these paths.

In Tibetan Buddhism, we are encouraged to seek not only personal freedom but also the achievement of enlightenment in order to help all other beings reach the same state. This is bodhichitta, the ultimate motivation, the most altruistic purpose ever conceived. To become so acquainted with bodhichitta that it becomes central to our thoughts, speech and action—well, *that* is a purpose worth cultivating, of infinite benefit to self and others.

MAKING BODHICHITTA OUR PRIMARY MOTIVATOR

We have opportunities each day to imprint our pets' minds—and our own—with the causes for future happiness. And given that bodhichitta is the ultimate key to happiness, the more frequently and authentically we remember this motivation, and remind our pets of it, the more powerful the benefits.

From a perspective of karma, any action motivated by bodhichitta becomes incomparably more powerful because of it. We are no longer simply concerned with positive everyday outcomes. We are directly creating the causes for our future enlightenment.

I have written much more about bodhichitta in my book, *Enlightenment To Go*, an introduction to the classic text by Shantideva, *A Guide to the Bodhisattva's Way of Life*. Shantideva writes many beautiful and powerful verses about the development of bodhichitta, but I will quote just one, in which he refers to it as an 'Awakening Mind':

All other virtues are like plantain trees;
For after bearing fruit, they simply perish.
Yet the perennial tree of the Awakening Mind
Unceasingly bears fruit and thereby flourishes without end.

Here, Shantideva explains one of the key advantages of bodhichitta: instead of positive actions producing positive results on a 'one-off' basis, like the fruit of the plantain, when those same actions are motivated by bodhichitta the benefits are never ending. Of all the methods for managing karma, bodhichitta is the most powerful.

YOU DON'T HAVE TO BELIEVE—JUST KEEP AN OPEN MIND

In the following pages, I outline a few suggestions about how to use the law of cause and effect to help create a better future for your pet, as well as yourself. Using the mindfulness described in previous chapters, we can start to exercise control of what happens in our mind. Motivated by bodhichitta, we deliberately cultivate specific practices to create the most powerful and favourable imprints on the consciousness of our pets.

If you are a relative newcomer to Buddhism, the concepts of karma and rebirth may seem frankly weird. Unbelievable, even.

And that's okay. You don't have to believe these things. They are not a part of our Western culture, and they take a while to become familiar with. I certainly found that to be the case in my own journey.

Fortunately, Buddhism isn't in the business of converting people, but instead offers tools to make us happier, whether that's happier atheists, Catholics, Jews or Nothing-in-particulars. Feel free to use those tools that make sense to you, and leave the others to one side. Just keep an open mind. Often it is the case that as our understanding of one subject deepens, it illuminates others in a quite unexpected way. Step by step, we discover an elegant coherence to all the practices.

A point worth emphasising is that even if Buddhism has it completely wrong about karma, even if there is no connection at all between what we do and think now, and what we experience in the future, and even if, when we die, our consciousness dies too, there is still a particular value in seeking the happiness of others: we feel happier too. And not in a superficial way.

The ancient Greeks used the word *eudemonia* to distinguish the profound wellbeing we experience through what we give to the world, from *hedonia*, the pleasure we get through what we take from it. The following pages are in *eudemonia* territory. The ancient Greeks would have agreed with Buddha that in giving to others, we, ourselves, are the first beneficiaries.

The last word on this subject goes to Buddha himself:

> Do not believe in anything simply because you have heard it. Do not believe in anything simply because it is spoken and rumored by many. Do not believe in anything simply because it is found written in your religious books. Do not believe in anything merely on the authority of your teachers and elders. Do not believe in traditions because they have been handed down for many generations. But after observation and analysis, when you find that anything agrees with reason and is conducive to the good and benefit of one and all, then accept it and live up to it.[3]

CREATING THE CAUSES FOR HAPPINESS

What are some of the practical ways we can help imprint our pets' minds with the causes for happiness, now and in the future?

RECOLLECTING BODHICHITTA

Pets entrain their minds with our own. Our paranormal is their normal. Exactly when and how they do this at any given moment may not be apparent, but a recurring wish, motivation and spoken phrase is something they are going to notice and become familiar with. If we choose the right context, and evoke a mental image of profound wellbeing as we do so, it is something to which they'll attach favourable associations. This is why giving voice to bodhichitta as much as possible, every single day, is one of the most profoundly beneficial things we can do for our pets. And given that animal intuition can be as much about an image or feeling as about words, offering the most benevolent visualisation at the same time may be useful. When I hug our cats, for example, I often visualise us both encompassed in a radiant, golden sphere of light, representing the bliss of enlightenment.

Giving our dog a hug in the morning, we can whisper to them: 'By this act of love may we become enlightened for the benefit of all living beings.' Opening a can of cat food, as we present it to our cat we can murmur: 'By this act of generosity may we become enlightened for the benefit of all living beings.' As we set out for a walk, brush a furry coat, offer a lap, or on any of the other positive contacts we have with our pets each day, we can repeat the bodhichitta motivation: 'By this . . . whatever positive thing it is . . . may we become enlightened for the benefit of all living beings.

Initially, this practice will feel contrived and even false: is hugging the dog really a cause for enlightenment? I was going to open the cat food anyway. And what is enlightenment, exactly?

The Dalai Lama explains the benefit of continuing nevertheless: 'Our bodhichitta may not yet be spontaneous. It is still something we have to fabricate. Nevertheless, once we have embraced and begun to develop this extraordinary attitude, whatever positive actions we do . . . while not appearing any different, will bring greatly increased results.'[4]

Bear in mind that 'love' as defined by Tibetan Buddhism is the wish to give happiness to others and 'compassion' is the wish to free others from suffering. These are useful, all-purpose definitions. So, for example, throwing a ball for the dog or taking the horse out on a favourite ride would both fall into the category of acts of love.

One of the reasons that bodhichitta is such a reality-changing concept is that it embodies pure, great love and pure, great compassion. 'Pure' is defined here as untainted by the expectation of receiving anything by way of return. 'Great' refers to the fact that we wish for all beings to experience happiness and wellbeing equally, not just the tiny circle of those on whom we usually focus our attention.

Little by little, as we become more familiar with bodhichitta as a motivation, we become more practised at applying it to our positive actions. It becomes habitual. Then we seek out opportunities to practise it, whether small, or more significant. It starts to shape our life, sometimes in quite unexpected ways. Eventually we start to become what we think.

Incidentally, while this advice is targeted mainly at helping pets, you can continue cultivating the habit even when your pets aren't physically present. Every trip to the bathroom becomes an act of purification. Every cup of coffee or nourishing meal can also be the cause to recollect our bodhichitta motivation.

Whatever the level to which our pets may understand, accept and relate to the concept of bodhichitta, the important point is that we are imprinting their mental continuum with a rare and transformative purpose. In so doing, we make it more likely that they will encounter bodhichitta again in a future lifetime. And when they do, it will attract their attention. If, as humans, they then decide to explore it for themselves, we have helped bestow on them the most priceless gift imaginable.

REPEATING MANTRAS

Mantra recitation is another powerful way we can help imprint the consciousness of our pet with the inner causes for transformation. As the story of Vasabandhu illustrates (see Chapter Three), simply hearing the recitation of sacred words was enough to propel a pigeon not only into a human lifetime, but one as a pre-eminent scholar.

The word 'mantra' comes from a Sanskrit term meaning 'mind protection'. Mantras consist of a number of syllables—usually in

Sanskrit, Tibetan or even a combination of languages—which embody a particular truth, meaning or insight. The benefits of repeating them can be understood on different levels.

At the first level, reciting a mantra gives our mind a virtuous object on which to focus. Recollecting the Buddhist definition of meditation—thoroughly familiarising the mind with virtue—when we repeat a mantra, we are doing exactly that. At the very least, we are protecting our own mind from non-virtue for the duration that we recite the mantra. And when we recite mantras aloud to our pets, we are helping familiarise *their* minds with an object of virtue too. The more we recite a mantra to them, the greater their familiarity.

At a second level, mantras offer a unique way to achieve spiritual insights. The literal meaning of mantras can seem fairly pedestrian. Take one of the most-recited mantras in Tibet, the mantra of Chenrezig, who is the Buddha of Compassion: *Om mani padme hum* (pronounced Om man-ee pad-me hung). In English this translates as 'Hail to the jewel of the lotus'. This literal translation is decidedly secondary to the symbolic representation, with each of the six syllables pointing to different levels of meaning, and separate pathways for contemplation. When we combine reciting a mantra with contemplating its meaning, we create the possibility of an 'aha' experience, through which our understanding of a particular subject deepens.

Perhaps we can articulate this shift in our perception or under-standing, perhaps not. The change may be non-conceptual but no less real—it may be that we have experienced our first taste of chocolate, metaphorically speaking. We use the same words as before to describe the flavours. But we are no longer just being theoretical. We know the truth of the meaning of the words and now we speak from personal experience.

At a third, more refined level, our most subtle mind is said to comprise two qualities—a knowingness and an energy. Mantra recitation not only impacts on the part of the mind that knows, as already described. The specific vibrational qualities of a mantra also influence the subtle energy of our mind, causing it to resonate in a particular and powerfully beneficial way.

As this aspect of the Dharma is esoteric, or hidden, a person is required to have received initiations for the full explanation and practices to be outlined. But it is useful to be aware that through mantra recitation we harness the prana, chi or life force referred to in other Eastern traditions.

It is my personal belief that it is this shift in our own energetic field that attracts pets to us when we meditate. Many animals are highly aware of the *quality* of our presence, and when this quality shifts to one of greater peace, benevolence and coherence, it draws them to us, as they seek to be close to us.

At a fourth level, when we recite a mantra, we connect to the qualities of the deity with whom the mantra is associated. Even if we have little understanding of the process in which we're engaged, when we do so with confidence in the outcome, we invest power in what we are doing. In the words of my teacher Zasep Tulku Rinpoche, 'It is not the words themselves that give mantras their power; it is the faith with which the words are recited.'[5]

Resonance may also shed light on the power of mantra recitation. By repeating a very specific ritual, we not only connect directly with those who have done the same thing in the past, but we benefit from their having done it.

What a gift to be able to offer our beloved pet—not only the warm contentment of the moment as we recite mantras to them but every mantra, recited with conviction, enabling us to draw on a collective reservoir of energy created by our forebears, including the greatest masters, and offering the karmic potential to germinate in the future, propelling both ourselves and our companion on the path to enlightenment.

MEDITATING REGULARLY

In the previous chapter (Chapter Six) I described the benefits of meditation in some detail. From the perspective of creating positive karma, if our pet comes to know meditation as a regular, natural and beneficial practice, we help create the causes for them to be drawn to the practice in the future, perhaps as humans. This is an extraordinary karmic imprint leading directly to the doorway for our pets' own future enlightenment. Motivated by bodhichitta, we can offer no greater service to our animal companions than this practice.

HANGING THANGKAS AND DISPLAYING STATUES AND OTHER SACRED OBJECTS

For those with an interest in Tibetan Buddhist practice, it is useful to have on the walls of our home 'thangkas', or wall-hangings, which display images of Shakyamuni, the historical Buddha, or other Buddhas, such as Chenrezig or Tara, a female Buddha of compassionate action. The more familiar a part of our lives they become, the stronger our disposition to them will be in the future (see the section on Buddhist deities on page 120).

Other Buddhist traditions have sacred objects which fulfil a similar purpose, such as the Gohonzon in some Japanese Buddhist traditions, as well as the sculptures, art and architecture of Zen.

Buddha statues are popular not only in many Buddhist traditions, but are now popular interior decorating items even among people with no special interest in Buddhism. The simple portrayal of a person in meditation can sometimes be enough to create a feeling of tranquillity in a room.

Because Westerners are unaware of the protocols about the correct placement of statues, we can get it spectacularly wrong from a Buddhist perspective. Within a ten-minute walk from my front door, for example, placed on the ground are Buddha statues in the front gardens or on the verandas of homes.

As an object of virtue and aspiration, Buddha should always be elevated, at least placed on a platform, raised bench or throne, or something that represents it. This is not such a difficult concept to understand: we would be unlikely to find the bust of Beethoven under the birdbath of a classical music lover—it would be positioned on a gleaming piano top or shelf to reflect its status.

We would also be unlikely to find a signed, framed jumper of a football great gathering dust on the garage floor of a sports fan.

In the same way, we need to give proper thought to the placement of Buddha statues, and recognise they are not simply an Eastern variant of the garden gnome! The reason to treat statues and other Buddha images with respect is not out of fear of offending Buddha or Buddhists—this is irrelevant—so much as the impact on our own minds as well as those of our loved ones. In the same way that aspiring sports people, artists or writers look to the heroes of their own traditions for inspiration, where we physically place representations of enlightenment should reflect the regard with which we hold our own ultimate objective.

AVOIDING THE CAUSES OF SUFFERING

PRACTICAL STEPS TO STOP AGGRESSION AND KILLING

One of the reasons why a small minority of people are cat haters is that our feline companions are often instinctive hunters. In Australia in particular, their killing of native fauna, some of which is endangered, is a cause for concern and even outrage. Some of the more vocal members of the anti-cat lobby seem to have lost sight of the fact that the only reason why humans have encouraged cats as pets for the past few thousand years is precisely because they are such effective hunters. We may, very recently, have changed our minds and decided that killing is no longer part of a cat's job description, but that's no reason to expect them to change their instincts in the evolutionary equivalent of an eye blink.

In time, change will occur. And some cats are clearly more persistent hunters than others. If you find your own pet is an enthusiast, take whatever practical steps may be needed. A bell around the neck is the usual way. Confining cats indoors, especially when they have been used to roaming, seems an unreasonably harsh restriction. Sensible, middle ground needs to be found if we are to help protect our cats from themselves and others.

From a causal perspective, killing is the cause for one's own life to be shortened, to endure a lower rebirth, experience disease, difficulties and violence, and to develop a tendency to enjoy killing, thereby perpetuating the vicious, downward spiral. Helping our pets to avoid unwittingly creating the karma of killing is therefore of tremendous value. As is the avoidance of aggression.

Here, the tendency for dogs to display belligerence is perhaps as common as prowling cats. But even if it is a tropical fish in your tank, you will be doing your companion a great service by taking practical measures to avoid placing it in a situation where it may behave with hostility—such as by putting too many fish in a tank.

DON'T ARGUE OR EXPOSE YOUR PETS TO VIOLENCE ON TELEVISION

One of my kind teachers, Zasep Tulku Rinpoche, offers the advice that exposure to aggression in the home is something we should avoid, for our pet's sake. 'Not in front of the children' was the very British cliché I grew up with, where parents were supposed to not provoke one another in the presence of their offspring. Well, the Buddhist equivalent might be 'Not in front of the pets'. Given their high sensitivity to mood and intention, a pet can become traumatised and stressed if it has to witness violence and confrontation.

We should even be sensitive to the impact of violent movies and TV shows when pets are present. Parental Guidance Advice is often offered, but PGA can mean something additional from a Dharma perspective. Loud, explosive sound, sirens, gunshot and screaming may be the dramatic finale of a movie that's had us engrossed for hours. But without any context, those same sounds may be highly stressful to those pets who dislike loud noises.

SHOULD I MAKE MY DOG OR CAT GO VEGAN?

Is eating meat creating bad karma for our cat or dog?

Importantly, any negative impact is mitigated by the fact that they have no say in what they are fed. Moreover, the digestive systems of cats and dogs are designed to process a meat-based diet; of course, dogs are more omnivorous, but they are still *Canis lupus familiaris*. Abrupt, enforced dietary changes on any animal can have dire consequences. We should not seek to impose our own behavioural beliefs on others, no matter how passionately held. And if we want to change our pet's diet radically, we should consult our vet first.

In the Tibetan Buddhist tradition, Tsong-Khapa—depicted on thangkas wearing a yellow hat and accompanied by his two students, Gyal Tseb Je and Khé Drub Je—is one of the most famous lamas. The three of them embody the qualities of wisdom, compassion and power—the implication being that all three of these are required to effect positive change. In the case of pet veganism, we may have the power to effect change, and wish to do so for reasons of compassion, but is it wise? My own view is that there are many other more important ways to help our pets, and reduce animal factory farming, than changing our pets' diets.

BUDDHIST DEITIES AND MANTRA RECITATION

Buddhism is a non-theistic tradition. Whether or not it can be termed a religion is debatable—the etymology of the word 'religion' refers to God. Many of us think of Buddhism as a practice-based psychology rather than a belief-based religion. Nevertheless, Buddhism has some of the outward trappings of a religion, such as temples, iconography, prayers and incense. Tibetan Buddhism also has deities. This opens up a world of confusion for Westerners, who may unwittingly impose preconceptions on what these deities represent.

Let's start with a blank canvas.

The main objective of Tibetan Buddhism is to help us attain enlightenment—Buddhahood—so that we can be of greatest benefit to all living beings. Enlightenment is a state beyond concept or description. How do you help people achieve something for which there are no words? Something that is multidimensional. And how do you make this accessible to people whether they are highly intelligent or not very bright, cerebral or passionate, practical or visionary, intense or laid back?

Part of the genius of Shakyamuni, the historical Buddha, was that he taught different and complementary versions of the Dharma to different audiences according to their temperament and abilities. Buddhism is not a 'one size fits all' tradition; you'll find a huge range of authentic Buddhist tools used by different people.

Among these practices in Tibetan Buddhism we find many deities. Shakyamuni Buddha is central to the tradition, but there are numberless millions of other Buddhas and bodhisattvas, or enlightened beings, some of whom are portrayed in statues and paintings representing specific qualities of enlightenment, such as compassionate action, energy, purification, healing, power, wisdom and so on.

If enlightenment is like a diamond, it may be seen as having many different facets. Each of the deities may be likened to a different facet. Trying to understand the nature of the whole diamond may be well beyond us initially, but we can focus on a particular facet. By drawing our minds close to a specific deity, we gain access to the whole diamond.

How do we draw close to a deity? One way is by reciting the mantra associated with that deity (see the previous section in this chapter on Repeating mantras). In reciting the mantra, we invoke the deity, opening up the possibility of accessing the qualities the deity represents.

Do these deities exist? Yes—in myriad manifestations. When we seek enlightenment we, ourselves, seek to manifest to benefit all beings—and countless people have become enlightened. Their many consciousnesses exist. They are out there wanting nothing more than to help us. But they are restricted in what they can do by our own karma.

We can shift that karma when we open ourselves directly to them through mantra recitation. This is like creating a metaphorical hoop which deities can hook onto, drawing us into their orbit of influence. The more we practise, the more different experiences we have of the deity, both while awake and in dream states. These experiences strengthen our confidence, empower our practice, and support our own non-conceptual experience of the mind of enlightenment.

Here are three mantras you may find useful:

1. The Buddha of Compassion/Chenrezig (Tibetan)/
Avalokiteshvara (Sanskrit)
His Holiness, the Dalai Lama, is believed by many Buddhists to be the manifestation of this Buddha.
Om Mani Padme Hum
Pronounced: *Om man-ee pad-me hung*

2. Tara/Female Buddha of Compassionate Action
Om Tare Tuttare Ture Soha
Pronounced: *Om tar-eh too-tar-eh too-ray so ha*

3. Medicine Buddha—for healing
Tayatha Om Bekadeze Bekadeze Maha Bekadze Bekadze Radza Samungate Soha

Pronounced: *Tie-ya-tar, Om beck-and-zay beck-and-zay ma-ha beck-and-zay beck-and-zay run-zuh sum-oon-gut-eh so-ha (The oon syllable to rhyme with the double 'o' in 'look').*

There are many online resources associated with each of these deities, including the pronunciation of their mantras. Spelling, pronunciations and even the mantras themselves may vary slightly depending on lineage, but toe-may-toe versus toe-mah-toe is of no great consequence. What's important is the attitude with which we recite a mantra, and the process of connection which deepens with each repetition.

CHAPTER EIGHT

HELPING OUR PETS ON THE PATH TO HEALING

Kathleen Prasad with Bruce Lee: 'By awakening our connectedness, Reiki cultivates compassion for others, which in turn brings about healing transformation.'

AMONG THE MOST ANXIOUS times for pet lovers is when one of our animal companions becomes ill. It can happen so unexpectedly, and the decline in our pet's health can be swift. One week it's situation normal, and the next, our cat or dog isn't eating and is barely able to move.

What we fear the most is that visit to the vet when we are presented with a serious or even terminal diagnosis. The harsh truth of impermanence becoming vividly real, we will do anything to help our pet through their illness—if such an outcome is possible. If not, we become achingly aware of the very limited time we have left with our loved one, and want to ensure that for however long it may be, they enjoy the best possible quality of life.

The purpose of this chapter is to offer suggestions about how we can help our pet in ways that complement whatever veterinary care they are receiving. It should perhaps go without saying that no vet is infallible, that the range of diagnostic options and treatments available are growing all the time, and that you shouldn't feel awkward about seeking a second opinion. It is also the case that the range of complementary treatments on offer is also expanding. Acupuncture, herbal and other naturopathic remedies are becoming more widely available, offering new healing modalities for animals.

After you've brought your pet home from the vet, the worst part for pet lovers is the feeling of helplessness. Apart from the obvious things, what else can you do? You'd give anything to make sure your pet is comfortable and to show them how much you love them. But you may regard your options as limited. You may even believe that you are somehow letting down a being whose dependence on you is total.

Fortunately, there *is* something you can do. Something that not only connects you and your pet on an immediate, intuitive level, but that, from a Buddhist perspective, is of greater ultimate value than any of the other things being done for them.

Buddhism offers very specific and powerful healing techniques. Practising these techniques can lead us to a way of reframing how we think about our pets and the nature of disease. Conducted with bodhichitta motivation, and with our pet as the focus of our attention, the truth is that we also benefit, any sense of helplessness being replaced by one of profound connection and benevolence. And of course, meditation can have a powerful impact on the physical recovery of our beloved companion too.

A HOLISTIC APPROACH TO MIND AND BODY

The words 'meditation' and 'medication' are just one letter different. The reason being that they both come from the same Latin root, *medeor*, meaning 'to heal'. 'Heal' also looks and sounds similar to 'whole' because they, too, have a shared source and meaning. Whether we meditate or medicate, we are seeking a return to healing or wholeness.

Why do we need to do this? What causes living beings to slip from ease to dis-ease in the first place?

Until recently, the focus of Western medicine was on repair rather than prevention and on material rather than energetic systems—the counterpoint to the Eastern approach. Genetic factors were also believed to hold the key to why some humans are more susceptible to certain illnesses than others. However, the Human Genome Project revealed that instead of the 120,000 plus genes humans were thought to possess, we have only 25,000—fewer than many animals, including even the humble sea urchin, and also many plants (rice has 38,000 genes). As cell biologist Bruce Lipton puts it: 'There are simply not enough genes to account for the complexity of human life or of human disease.'[1]

Instead of single genes or small gene groups being associated with certain conditions, the reality is very much more complex. This has given rise to the field of epigenetics, which examines how and why genes are 'switched' on or off and, importantly, the impact of lifestyle and mental factors on physical wellbeing.

There is no reason to believe why this same interplay of mental and physical wellbeing isn't as true for our pets as it is for us.

According to people engaged in the growing mind–body movement, physical disease is a manifestation of a disturbance of the mind. Our bodies don't become ill, *we* become ill. Removing or repairing the physical symptoms of disease—narrow arteries, a tumour, inflamed joints—will be to little avail if we don't also remove or repair the original cause of those symptoms in our consciousness.

By way of illustration, if we were driving along in our car and an unknown warning light suddenly appeared on the dashboard, chances are we'd take our car into a service centre to have it looked at. We'd realise that something was amiss and needed urgent attention.

If, while at the service centre, we saw a mechanic reach behind the dashboard, remove the offending light globe, and tell us that our problem was solved, well, even the least practical among us would see through that. Removing the warning light doesn't fix the problem. It only removes the evidence that a problem exists.

In just the same way, treating the physical manifestation of disease, even successfully, does not equal treating the disease itself. Unless we look beyond the warning globe of sickness and deal with the underlying reason for it appearing, we risk far greater problems down the road.

This analogy is offered by authors Thorwald Dethlefsen and Ruediger Dahlke, MD, in their book, *The Healing Power of Illness*, which tells us: 'Illness is not some accidental, and therefore disagreeable upset along the way, but the very way itself along which people can progress towards wholeness. The more consciously we can think about that way, the more likely is it to lead us to the goal. Our purpose is not to resist illness but to use it.'[2]

True healing, according to this view, must occur at the level of consciousness.

There is already ample evidence showing the negative impact of stress on physical wellbeing, whether human or animal. People who feel lonely and those who are pessimistic have been shown in separate studies to have significantly more compromised immune systems, suffer from higher blood pressure and be more likely to experience heart disease.[3] There is no reason to believe that the same basic principle—that mind and body form a systemic whole—doesn't also apply to animals. Along with growing evidence about the harmful impact of negative mental states on the body, there is also substantial evidence of the opposite—specifically, that meditative states promote physical healing.

In the past two decades in particular, a huge amount of research has been carried out establishing the powerful and measurable impacts of meditation on a large number of metrics which reflect our wellbeing. I provide a full description of these in my book *Why Mindfulness Is Better Than Chocolate*. Meditation has been shown to lower high blood pressure, reduce other stress markers and help treat heart disease. It boosts our immune systems, slows the ageing process, manages chronic pain and helps with inflammatory conditions. It also plays a role at an epigenetic level in preventing the expression of genes associated with serious illnesses, including cancer. In terms of psychological benefits, people who meditate regularly have greater emotional resilience; are less susceptible to depression, anxiety and loneliness; and their brains become rewired to be happier. There can be little doubt that if the benefits of meditation were available in capsule form, it would be the biggest selling drug of all time.

While meditation may be a powerful way for *us* to heal, to become whole, what is the evidence that we can promote healing in our pets by including them when we meditate? Empirical evidence has yet to be gathered, but there is a wealth of anecdotal evidence, in particular from those who practise reiki with animals.

Reiki comes from the Japanese words 'rei' meaning spirit and 'ki' meaning energy—in other words, 'spiritual energy'. The practice of reiki in relation to animals can simply involve meditating with pets. There is no need to position oneself in a particular way, or to place your hands near or upon a pet. It is, rather, a matter of sitting quietly with an animal, and inviting that animal to be a part of one's meditation, as described earlier in this book.

Frans and Bronwen Stiene are highly regarded reiki researchers, practitioners, teachers and authors who have spent much time in Japan studying traditional practices. Establishing the International House of Reiki in New South Wales, they have done much to translate the spirituality and practices of this tradition into a form that Westerners can relate to (see: http://www.ihreiki.com). This includes using reiki to help heal animals.

Kathleen Prasad, a California-based reiki teacher and author, who studied with the Stienes, has focused her reiki practice on animals, with the main emphasis being its healing power (see: www.animalreikisource. com). Using reiki to treat herself in 1998, she noticed how her dog Dakota was so drawn to her that he came to sit on her feet. She realised that Dakota tuned into the healing power of reiki without her needing to explicitly give it to him. As she puts it, 'It was as if he was already fluent in a language much too subtle for me to sense.'

In Australia, Carolyn Trethewey is a leading advocate of animal reiki, working with a growing number of vets and animal rescue centres, and introducing the gentle power of meditation to many pets and their human companions (see: http://pausehq.com.au).

The combined experiences of these practitioners over countless interactions, as well as that of meditators from a variety of other backgrounds, has shown us that meditating with animals can contribute to healing in a number of important ways.

HOW MEDITATING CAN ASSIST IN HEALING OUR PETS

ENABLES SELF-REPAIR EVEN WHEN WE DON'T KNOW THE PRECISE CAUSE OF DISEASE

As pet lovers we can get anxious and frustrated when we don't know exactly what's wrong with our pet. Although increasingly sophisticated diagnostic aids are becoming available to vets, sometimes not even these can pinpoint precisely the cause of a pet's sickness. What's more, they may be so expensive that they're out of financial reach, presenting pet lovers with the added dilemma of feeling guilty about not being able to afford to provide for their loved one.

Alternatively, it may be the case that, whatever diagnostics are carried out, the treatment options remain the same, so there is little point putting our animal companion through the trauma of yet another visit to the vet, anaesthesia, invasive procedures and post-operative pain for the sake of information that can't be acted upon.

Meditating offers a completely different healing modality, giving our pets the best opportunity for self-repair, by providing the optimal context in which this can happen.

Carolyn Trethewey, of Pause, relates the story of Saba, a cocker spaniel, whose owner, Verity, was distraught. Saba had a serious spleen problem (ITP) and the vet believed that surgery would be needed.

However, there was a problem: part of the spleen's role is to store platelets but instead of storing the platelets, Saba's body was destroying them. Until her platelet levels increased significantly, surgery was just too high a risk. What's more, she wasn't responding to the medicine she had been given to boost platelet production. Saba remained under round-the-clock observation at the clinic—in itself a cause of stress both to her and to Verity.

Carolyn offered to visit Saba. When she did, she immediately noticed how subdued and weak she seemed. Carolyn also took in the bright lights, powerful odours and general busyness of the clinic. Finding a quiet corner, she and Verity sat meditating with Saba—Carolyn offering Verity a simple, breathing meditation to practise. In her heart, Carolyn sought to communicate a simple message to Saba to let go of the lights and odours and noise of the vet clinic, as well as her own feelings of weakness.

Sitting together in silence, after some minutes, Saba settled next to her owner Verity, and fell asleep. Verity commented to Carolyn that Saba seemed more relaxed than she had been for a long while.

After the session, Carolyn left, and Saba went back to her cage. Verity later told her that Saba slept for fourteen hours straight. When she woke up the vet tested her platelet levels. They had returned to normal. After further diagnosis, the vet determined that no surgery would be required either. Saba was free to go home.

Dr Herbert Benson of Harvard Medical School was the first to draw attention to the body's ability to self-repair—if we give it the right conditions. Meditation is a state that optimises those conditions. It seems that when we meditate with pets, through their habit of entraining their minds with ours, they are able to benefit from whatever calmness and compassion we can offer. They appear capable of resonating with these same qualities themselves, and self-healing is promoted, irrespective of the nature or location of the disease from which they have been suffering.

SPEEDS UP HEALING, INCLUDING AFTER SURGERY

Dr Benson first came to understand the power of meditation to promote self-repair when observing patients recovering from heart attacks. Those who practised meditation recovered significantly more quickly than those who didn't. 'The relaxation response', as he labelled it, not only helped patients enjoy greater levels of equanimity and wellbeing, it also accelerated self-repair. Our bodies can be highly effective at repairing themselves, as long as we provide them with the right circumstances to do so.

The same holds true of pets. When they are provided with optimised conditions, they too recover more quickly from illness and surgery. Meditating with them provides a powerfully beneficial context in which to aid their swift recovery. When we meditate with our pets, we help them enjoy positive mental states, including love, trust and wellbeing. The biological impact of these states is to increase the oxytocin in the body, a hormone that reduces stress and increases happiness, to multiply white blood cells, which help fight infection, and to bolster their immune defences. Meditating before surgery can help ensure the operation is more effective and meditating afterwards can help speed up healing.

As Kathleen Prasad puts it so beautifully: 'By awakening this connectedness, Reiki cultivates compassion for others, which in turn brings about healing transformation.'

HELPS RELIEVE PAIN

Meditation is becoming more widely accepted as a pain-management method, especially for people who experience recurring or chronic pain, and sometimes in cases where all other options have been exhausted.

While it may seem counter-intuitive that increased focus can reduce the sensation of pain, there are different methods by which meditation can help us dissociate from feelings of pain—the pain signals are still being communicated, but we can turn down the volume. This pain-muting effect continues after a meditation session has ended. And, importantly, it is readily available even to those who have never meditated before—you don't have to be a Zen master for it to work.

Anecdotal evidence suggests that animals, too, appear in less pain after spending time with a meditator than before. The same process of dissociation from pain seems to occur, and perhaps closer association with the positive state engendered through meditation, providing relief, comfort and enhanced feelings of wellbeing.

This question opens out to a broader one: is our pets' experience of pain the same or different from ours? Similar neural pathways and activity may be present, but as alluded to above, the way in which we pay attention to pain can significantly alter our experience of its intensity.

It is also the case that we humans tend to overlay the experience of pain with cognitive activity that complicates and magnifies our suffering. A case of toothache can lead to thoughts like: the dentist is going to have to give me an injection and I hate those—they are agonising! This will probably lead to root-canal work—I'm looking at weeks of trauma! Dental bills are massively expensive—so much for my holiday plans! This is a truly awful financial blow! My clients/boss/colleagues will hate me for being away right now and leaving them in the lurch—talk about a career-limiting crisis! I'm going to be a dribbling mess for the rest of the day—when Adam from accounts stops by this afternoon he'll think I'm a shambles!

And so it goes on. By the time we have really worked up a negative head of steam, it's hard to know how much our sense of existential angst is caused by the pain in our mouth, and how much by the thoughts about the pain in our mouth.

Do pets have similar cognition? We can't know for sure, but observation suggests not. A relative absence of narrative chatter would imply that animals' awareness of the here and now is generally greater than that of humans. This may mean that they tend not to overlay negative cognition onto physical pain. It could also mean that they are more available to our influence as meditators.

I have often had an intuitive feeling that my pets use mindfulness or meditation as a form of pain management. Having no access to paracetamol or other pain-killers, unlike us they can't just head for the bathroom cabinet and pop a pill if they get a headache. All they are left with is their mind—and perhaps the possibility of disassociating from pain as much as possible?

We know that cats sometimes purr to cope with pain and to promote healing. Whether or not this occurs instinctively or through conscious choice is something we're not currently clear about. But whether instinctive or innate, vets often remark about the high levels of stoicism shown by many pets in the face of discomfort and pain that would reduce humans to a state of abject misery. This stoicism can only be enhanced if we are able to offer not only pharmacological solutions, but also a presence of compassion, trust and love.

REDUCES THE SIDE EFFECTS OF TREATMENT

Many of us have experienced the side effects of medical treatment. Whether it's the constipation sometimes caused by pain-killers, or the more serious and global side effects associated with chemotherapy such as nausea, mouth sores, hair loss and fatigue, we have all witnessed if not personally experienced what happens when our bodies recover from medical intervention.

Among the many clinical studies of meditation in recent years has been its impacts on the recovery journeys of patients. As has been observed many times since Dr Herbert Benson, meditation has been shown both to enhance and speed up the recovery process, as well as to reduce the sometimes harmful impact of side effects, in quite profound ways.

Controlled studies have shown how meditation in humans helps lower stress symptoms, fatigue and feelings of nausea, and improves mood, energy levels and immune function among patients being treated with chemotherapy.[4]

The same trends have been observed when meditating with pets. Their ability to get over sessions at the animal hospital or clinic, and return to a state of wellbeing, is enhanced.

There is a further benefit for those animals who are highly reactive. Their temperaments may be such that they are naturally highly strung, restless or agitated, or visits to the vet may make them more anxious and perturbed than usual—the very opposite state from the one in which healing happens. But meditating with animals who are behaving like this can settle them, for at least the duration of the session, enabling them to get into self-repair mode and into the most conducive state, when the impact of the traditional treatment can be optimised.

As Kathleen Prasad observes, 'Through the mindful presence that Reiki meditation cultivates, we can more easily navigate our life's challenges with grace and surrender while we learn to listen to and be present for animals in a compassionate space. In this way we learn to share precious moments of healing with them.'

OFFERS PSYCHOLOGICAL AS WELL AS PHYSICAL HEALING

Returning to wholeness may be as much about healing the mind as the body. Carolyn Trethewey relates the story of a visit to the Cat Haven in the Perth suburb of Shenton Park, where she regularly meditates with cats who find themselves there for a variety of reasons.

On occasion Carolyn may be asked to meditate with a particular cat, and one day a staff member asked her to sit with a cat called Finlay who was showing a lot of aggression. The Cat Haven has a proactive approach to finding homes for cats, using social media highly effectively. But not even the cutest Facebook posting was going to lead to a 'furrever home' for Finlay if he continued to lash out angrily at visitors.

The condos in which the cats are housed include an open area, a toilet area and a private section where cats can go if they don't wish to be disturbed. Arriving at Finlay's condo, Carolyn saw he was in the private section. When she tentatively opened the door, he reacted by arching his back and baring his teeth angrily, his fur standing on end.

She closed the door immediately, and found a place to meditate just outside his condo. Given the strength of the reaction she had just encountered, she had no great expectation that her session would have any impact. But she could try.

Carolyn has a sense that the pet she is with 'connects' when she feels her meditation deepen. And that was exactly what happened during the session that followed. Sitting on the other side of the door from Finlay, she continued to meditate, evoking a peaceful mind–body state.

After about fifteen minutes an image suddenly came to mind. It was of a cat wrapped in a sheet or blanket being swung around and around like a lasso. She had no doubt where the image came from, suggesting the horrifying cause of Finlay's trauma. The cruelty of it shocked her. But having acknowledged it, she let it go, and continued to hold onto the peaceful state. She meditated for another quarter of an hour before ending. And, curious though she was to open the door again to Finlay, she intuitively felt it would be better to simply slip away.

When she got to the Cat Haven the following week, the same staff member who had asked her to sit with Finlay told her he had become a completely different cat. Since her last visit, he had been friendly and purring. Such a delight, in fact, that he had been taken home by a new family.

'Finlay was ready to let go of that experience,' observes Carolyn. 'Animals can do this much more quickly than we can. Sometimes all it takes is our compassionate presence for them to be able to let go of past hurts, and be ready to move on with their lives. Animals' past experiences can and do impact them deeply and just as we are sometimes just not ready to let go of something yet, it's the same for the animals. Finlay was ready, and in doing so his connection to his centre, to who he really is, was deepened strongly. It is a testament to animals that they are able to let go a lot more easily than humans do—this is one of the many lessons they are here to teach us.'

This story accords with the psychological or energetic shifts we have already noted in previous chapters. Returning to wholeness is as much a matter of mind as it is of body. Providing our pets with the space and state in which to let go is one of the special services we can offer when we meditate with them.

HELPS OUR PETS WHEN PHYSICAL HEALING ISN'T POSSIBLE

There can come a point when we're out of options, or the options available will do little to prolong the quality, as well as the quantity, of our pet's life. Sometimes this point is clearly signposted. At other times it is a recognition that evolves over a period of several days or more. The time may come when we realise that allowing our pet a natural death may be a wiser and more compassionate choice than further intervention and prolonged suffering.

Having set out to help achieve full physical recovery for our pet, as well as the elimination of whatever mental origins of disease may exist, have we failed? Does this mean that healing meditation does not work? Or that our concentration isn't good enough for it to work? These important questions are sometimes asked and they deserve to be answered.

It may be that your pet's karma is so strong that you don't have the power to alter the course of the physical disease. Because we are born as sentient beings on planet earth, we all have the karma to die. That karma may be what your pet is currently dealing with, just as, in our own time, we will all die of something too, no matter how accomplished we may become as meditators.

But this doesn't mean that our meditation has been a waste of effort. Every time we sit to meditate with our pet, we are creating new, positive causes for future positive effects in their mind stream, as well as our own. We are helping purify negativities that have the potential to lead to future illness and suffering, and are mitigating—and, who knows, maybe even completely removing—the cause that triggered the onset of this particular disease.

If our purpose is not to help our pets resist illness, but to use the illness as a means of progressing to wholeness, then there can be fewer more powerful ways to respond to disease than by using it as the means to deepen a meditation practice. If we assume a more panoramic perspective, rather than one focusing on immediate outcomes in this lifetime alone, we can give our pet no greater gift than meditation in their final days, weeks or months. Even when physical recovery is no longer an option, the opportunity for them to approach their final transition with a mind influenced by love and compassion is the most extraordinarily precious and rare privilege we can bestow. We are offering them a direct cause for their own future enlightenment.

HEALING MEDITATIONS

It is not necessary to learn a specific meditation to help your pet through illness. As animal reiki practitioners have demonstrated, simply being present with an open heart is enough to provide a healing context for your pet.

What's more, even if you are a complete newcomer to meditation, you should not underestimate the impact your meditation is having. Starting out, your subjective experience may be that your thoughts are all over the place and you may question the benefits of what you are doing. But the measurable, scientific reality is that meditation profoundly changes body and mind. When we meditate with our pet, this shift in state affects them too.

There is, in Tibetan Buddhism, a range of meditations developed specifically for healing, both ourselves and others. I share two of these below, and you may like to try them out. If you like one in particular, or you feel your pet is really benefiting, stick with it. If you like two or three of the meditations shared in this book, feel free to rotate them. The effect of using different meditations is a bit like using different gym equipment. Their combined use can offer great, holistic benefit. What's important is not to switch mid-way through a session, but always stick with one particular meditation type for the duration of each session in order to deepen familiarity and develop concentration.

TAKING AND GIVING MEDITATION (TONG LEN)

Tong len is a foundational meditation in Tibetan Buddhism in which we envision taking away the suffering of others and giving them happiness. There are many different versions of this meditation. The following is a very simple version, and no less powerful because of that.

Adopt the optimal meditation posture—remember to keep a straight back.

Take a few deep breaths and exhale. As you do, imagine you are letting go of all thoughts, feelings and experiences. As far as possible try to be pure consciousness, abiding in the here and now.

Begin your meditation with the following motivation:

> By the practice of this meditation, may NAME of PET and all living beings be immediately, completely and permanently purified of all disease, pain, sickness and suffering.
> May this meditation be a direct cause for us to attain enlightenment,
> For the benefit of all living beings without exception.

Focusing on your in-breaths, imagine that you are inhaling radiant, white light. This light represents healing, purification, balance and blissful energy. Imagine it filling your body, until every cell is completely permeated with it. Keep on breathing like this, with the focus on the qualities of the light that you inhale.

After some minutes, change the focus of your attention to your exhalations. Visualise that you exhale a dark, smoke-like light. The darkness represents whatever pain, illness or potential for illness, negativity of body, speech or mind you experience. With each out-breath imagine you are able to release more and more of this negativity. Keep on breathing like this, with the focus on the qualities of the light that you exhale.

After some minutes, combine the two, so that you are both letting go of negativity and illness as well as breathing in radiant wellbeing.

Now that you have some practice, imagine that you are inhaling and exhaling these qualities on behalf of your pet/s. Whatever you breathe in, you direct into their being. Whatever you exhale, you do so on their behalf. You are a conduit for healing energy, and for letting go of all suffering.

Make this the main focus of your meditation session—the taking away of your pet's sickness and suffering and the giving of purification, healing and wellbeing. You may decide to assign, say, three or four breaths to each of the following qualities to give structure to your meditation:

In-breaths	Out-breaths
Taking in healing energy	Getting rid of all physical and mental disease
Complete purification/cleansing/ healing	All physical sickness/pain/ suffering
Radiant wellbeing—energy and vitality	All mental negativity/distress/ anxiety
Peace, balance, mental tranquillity	Hatred, craving and all delusions

In-breaths	Out-breaths
Love and compassion	

End the session as you began:

> By the practice of this meditation, may NAME of PET and all living beings be immediately, completely and permanently purified of all disease, pain, sickness and suffering.
> May this meditation be a direct cause for us to attain enlightenment,
> For the benefit of all living beings without exception.

MEDICINE BUDDHA MEDITATION

If you are a newcomer to Medicine Buddha, you can find an image of him on my blog, under the category, Medicine Buddha (www. davidmichie.com). In the same blog I have also provided a link to a video showing how to pronounce his mantra as well as other resources. I suggest you become acquainted with both the visualisation and the mantra before trying out the meditation.

Adopt the optimal meditation posture—remember to keep a straight back.

Take a few deep breaths and exhale. As you do, imagine you are letting go of all thoughts, feelings and experiences. As far as possible try to be pure consciousness, abiding in the here and now.

Begin your meditation with the following motivation:

By the practice of this meditation, may NAME of PET and all living beings be immediately, completely and permanently purified of all disease, pain, sickness and suffering.

May this meditation be a direct cause for us to attain enlightenment,

For the benefit of all living beings without exception.

Visualise Medicine Buddha sitting facing you, at about the height of your forehead, a few metres in front of you. Don't worry if your visualisation isn't great. An orb of dark blue light will suffice. If you struggle with that, even his imagined presence is enough. The more real you can make it, the better. Try to get into the way of thinking that if you were to raise your eyes/open your eyes, you would find yourself looking directly into his.

Recollect the key visual elements of Medicine Buddha—his radiant, lapis lazuli blue-coloured body is the symbol of healing energy. The medicine plant he is holding in his right hand, and bowl of purifying nectar he is holding in his lap with his left hand, both reflect the healing power of his presence.

Going beyond the visual, try to imagine how his presence would *feel*. If you have ever experienced the presence of His Holiness the Dalai Lama, this may suggest something to you. Sometimes Medicine Buddha is described as being everything beautiful dissolved into one. Imagine he is gazing at you and your pet/s with more love than a mother for her only child. His is an incredibly powerful, compassionate being and when you invoke him, you should feel that he is definitely in your presence, wanting nothing more than to help you and those you care for.

Recite his mantra:

Tayatha Om Bekadeze Bekadeze Maha Bekadze Bekadze Radza Samungate Soha

Pronounced: *Tie-ya-tar, Om beck-and-zay beck-and-zay ma-ha beck-and-zay beck-and-zay run-zuh sum-oon-gut-eh so-ha (The 'oon' syllable to rhyme with the double 'o' in 'look').*

In general, mantras should be whispered so that only you can hear them. But when reciting this mantra for your pet's benefit, I suggest you murmur or whisper it loud enough for them to hear.

Keep repeating the mantra.

Once you are familiar with the mantra, build in the visualisation of blue healing lights and nectars radiating from Medicine Buddha's heart. These flow directly through the crown of your head into your body, and also into the body of your pet. You and your pet are now filled with the most powerful healing energy. Visualise this endless outpouring of radiant, healing light, while continuing the mantra recitation.

As you recite the mantra, it is useful to visualise specific results with each mantra, or perhaps cycles of three or four mantras, such as:

Removal of all pain and suffering
Healing of all physical disease
Eliminating all mental afflictions and distress
Purifying all possible future causes of disease
Bestowing of energy and robust good health
Abundance of happiness, love and compassion

As with most meditations, the more personal and direct you can make your meditation the better. So if you know your rabbit has kidney problems, direct at least some of your focus to healing her kidneys. You don't need to be an anatomical expert for this. It is more about intentionality and directing your thoughts for this specific purpose. Holistic healing is also very useful for the reason explained at the start of this chapter—that is, beneath the physical manifestation the cause in consciousness can also be addressed.

For some periods you may wish simply to focus on the visualisation, and give the mantra recitation a break. Or vice versa. Try to keep as fresh as possible the collective practice of the strongly imagined presence of Medicine Buddha, the visualisation of healing lights and nectars, and the mantra recitation.

Continue like this until you end the session as you began:

By the practice of this meditation, may NAME of PET and all living beings be immediately, completely and permanently purified of all disease, pain, sickness and suffering.

May this meditation be a direct cause for us to attain enlightenment,

For the benefit of all living beings without exception.

If you are especially drawn to Medicine Buddha meditation, you may like to buy mala beads—like a rosary—and set yourself the objective of completing, say, one, three, five or seven rounds of mantras in each session. A mala typically has 108 beads, but this is counted as 100, allowing leeway for mispronunciations, inattention and so on.

THE FORCE IS WITH YOU!

When practising a healing meditation, no matter how uncertain or tentative you may feel to begin with, there is no need to feel helpless or inadequate; there is a lot more going on than meets the eye. Not only is the material world less solid than it appears, and more illusion-like than we may comprehend, but matter is also energy—our thoughts, speech and actions have an energetic quality to them. When channelled in a skilful way, and used to invoke other unseen and incredibly powerful energetic forces, like those of Medicine Buddha, we are more than one person sitting alone in a room with a sick pet. Instead we become a conduit for healing energy and benevolent purpose greater than we can possibly comprehend.

RESONANCE AND THE POWER OF MEDITATION

Resonance is a fascinating concept, especially for those who practise meditation-mantra recitation in particular. The term offers a possible explanation for how memory and habit become engrained in nature.

It has been shown that actions undertaken in the past become easier and more effective for different living beings to carry out in the future. For example, if rats are taught a new trick in a laboratory in Los Angeles, rats in laboratories in other parts of the world generally learn that same new trick more quickly. The more people who practise a new skill, like windsurfing, the easier it becomes for others who come to windsurfing to learn that skill.

A good example is the Flynn Effect. Over time, people score higher and higher on standard IQ tests. Average scores of 100 rise steadily over a period of years. There is no indication that people are becoming more intelligent, merely that they are getting better at doing those particular tests. When the tests are revised, as they are periodically, scores once again return to 100.

The theory of resonance suggests that when we do something that has been done before, we become linked, through an organising pattern of influence, or a field, to others who have done the same thing. We resonate with them. Like other fields—electric, magnetic, radiation—the field may be invisible, but its effects are not. And it reaches over time and space.

What happens when we recite a mantra that has been repeated by millions of people for thousands of years? We bring ourselves into resonance with them. We benefit from their cumulative influence, just as we contribute to that influence ourselves.

As we sit in our room reciting mantras, we may be physically alone or with our pet, but in a different way we are tuning into an influence and community, an energetic field reaching back through the centuries to include everyone else in our tradition.

CHAPTER NINE

SUPPORTING OUR PETS THROUGH DEATH AND BEYOND

Gail Pope, Founder of BrightHaven and pioneer of the animal hospice movement, with Joey. 'There is no greater gift in life than to be present during the hospice time as well as at the end of this beautiful journey, to share love with another, and most especially to do so with courage and grace.'

IN THE WEST MOST of us do our best not only to avoid dying but even to think about it. Our culture doesn't encourage us to think about death. From the perspective of materialism, arguably still the dominant belief system because brain and consciousness are seen as synonymous, the end of one equals the end of the other. Contemplating death may have value in helping us appreciate the preciousness of life. But that aside, there is little to be gained from focusing on the process, the mechanics of dying.

From the perspective of that other, significant cultural influence, Christianity, death is closely followed by an ascent to heaven, descent to hell or perhaps a period in purgatory. These outcomes will not be changed by the way in which we die—although it's interesting that Roman Catholicism encourages the use of anointing and *viaticum*— Latin for 'with you on the way', to prepare the soul for what lies ahead.

When it comes to our beloved pets, their spiritual fate remains a subject of even more confusion and conjecture. Popular psychics assure us that every pet crosses the Rainbow Bridge, where we'll find them waiting when our time comes to pass. Materialists hold little truck with such sentiment. Meanwhile, the range of views in Christianity is striking, largely because of debate about how the word 'soul' should be interpreted: does it mean life force? Or does it refer to immortality? And can these both refer to all sentient beings or only to one species?

Mixed messages and general bewilderment, not to mention the fact that losing everyone and everything we hold dear is a gloomy prospect, makes it easier to simply put the whole subject out of mind. To focus on what is more immediately ahead of us. And when death rears its ugly head, to frame it as a medical, veterinary or undertaking matter, outsource it to the experts and move on swiftly.

Buddhism approaches the subject of dying from a radically different perspective. For the past 2500 years, across all its many and varied branches, the Buddhist view of the death process has remained consistent. It has also been an important subject of teaching, discussion and meditative preparation.

As far as Buddhists are concerned, death is not an ending, but rather a time of major—and even rather exciting—transition. Our state of mind at that time of transition can be significant in determining not only what happens in the immediate future. It may also provide the framework for our whole experience of reality for another lifetime.

The implications of this view are significant for pet lovers because they suggest that the *way* in which our pets die, does matter; that we need not be helpless bystanders but can perform a vitally important role; and, significantly, for seven weeks after the physical death of our animal companion, we can continue to undertake valuable activities for our pet's ultimate wellbeing.

To understand how all this may be the case, it is helpful to have an overview of the nature of consciousness, how our experience of reality arises and, in particular, the way in which we can influence our pets during and after the death process for the best possible outcome.

THE NATURE OF CONSCIOUSNESS

The view of Buddhism is that humans and animals are equal in possessing a mind that, as described earlier (see Chapter Three), may be defined as *a formless continuum of clarity and cognition.*

One of our biggest challenges, as Westerners, is letting go of the preconceptions we have about what exactly it is that may move through different lifetimes. So conditioned by both Christianity and, ironically, materialism, about this entity known as the soul, we have a tendency to think that our acquired personality, together with memories, likes and dislikes, the ego and all its kit and caboodle, are what Buddhists suggest is transferred wholesale from one body to the next.

This is not the Buddhist view.

Even we beginner meditators can come to recognise, after a while, that consciousness exists at different levels. Those aspects of personality and memories, which we may have come to believe are part of some concrete, independent entity called 'me', turn out to be nothing more than ideas. Notions that come and go, with no fixity at all. There is no self, apart from the concept of a self. And that concept is constantly being revised. Meat-eaters become vegans, left-wing students become conservative politicians, and the most hard-nosed capitalists become warm-hearted philanthropists, as we redefine our ideas about the world, and who we are.

These ideas may be likened to clouds passing through the sky. The clouds are the narrative chatter constantly arising, which changes depending on our mood, or the company we keep, or a thousand other things. With practice we can learn to acknowledge, accept and let go of this often needless, running commentary. Instead we focus on what endures: the sky through which it passes.

It is the sky-like mind which is the formless continuum of clarity and cognition. It is this subtle consciousness that Buddhists say moves from one life to the next. This is one of the reasons that Buddhism is sometimes called 'the Middle Way', because it suggests an option between eternalism on the one hand and nihilism on the other.

This is also how it is entirely possible that subtle consciousness could experience reality as a human at one time, and a dog or cat at another. We are not talking about the transfer of cognitive complexity, intelligence, a hard-drive of memory or other aspects of mental functioning. What remains after the body and brain have shut down at the end of a particular lifetime, whether animal or human, is merely a formless continuum of clarity and cognition. And it is propelled by the conditioning we have created, or karma.

HOW REALITY ARISES

We usually assume that reality is happening 'out there', independent of our body and mind, and that we observe and interact with it. But even at a neuroscientific level that model was abandoned in the last century.

To use the cognitive visual system as an example, it is now known that some 80 per cent of fibres in the part of the brain that processes visual imagery come from the cortex—which governs functions including memory—and only 20 per cent from the retinas. As Professor Gregory, one of the United Kingdom's most eminent neuropsychologists, says: 'We carry in our heads predictive hypotheses of the external world of objects and of ourselves. These brain-based hypotheses of perceptions are our most immediate reality. But they entail many stages of physiological signalling and complicated cognitive computing so *experience is but indirectly related to external reality* [my italics].'

Neuroscience shows that perceptions may be up to 90 per cent memory and, as Professor Gregory puts it: 'This startling notion that perception is projecting brain-hypotheses outwards into the physical world—endowing the world with colour and sound and meaning—has surprising implications.'[1]

It is not only neuroscientists who reveal that our experience of reality is the opposite of what we might expect. Quantum scientists have done so too. As Austrian physicist, Erwin Schrödinger, put it: 'Every man's world picture is and always remains a construct of his mind and cannot be proved to have any other existence.'[2]

Two and a half thousand years before Erwin Schrödinger and quantum science, Buddha said the same thing even more simply: 'The objective world arises from the mind itself.' I prefer Buddha's version, because he doesn't specify whether the mind belongs to a man, a woman, a dog or a parakeet!

The idea that we create our own sense of reality is worthy of thought and reflection. If our world arises from our mind, we can change the world by changing our mind. Those things that we choose to pay attention to, to believe in, to focus energy on, become our reality. They may not be others' reality. We may walk down the same street as other beings, even share the same bed as them, but the way that flowers smell, buildings look, noises sound and others seem is patently different for each one of us, in ways which may be subtly nuanced, or dramatically different.

The reality we experience is propelled by the causes we have created. And as discussed in Chapter Seven, on guiding our pets towards a positive future, if our goal is to help them experience the most positive reality possible, we should cultivate the habit of recollecting bodhichitta, practising pure, great love and pure, great compassion, and saying mantras to connect or resonate with beings more enlightened than ourselves. The more habitual, instinctive or automatic this becomes, the better.

This is important not only in life, but especially during the death process, which I will outline, before suggesting the practical steps we can take to best help our pet make a peaceful and positive transition.

THE PROCESS OF DYING

Just as our experiences of life are unique to each one of us, death is too. Each one of us—whether we are human, dog, lamb or other being—experiences the reality of our physical dissolution somewhat differently.

Tibetan Buddhism provides a description of the death process for humans, comprising four stages of physical dissolution, followed by four stages of mental dissolution, taking us to the most subtle state of experience, known as the clear light of death. As Buddhists, we rehearse this experience on a regular basis. That said, it's important to emphasise that this is an indicative model, and each of us will experience dying in our own way.

It's not unusual for a dying person to report the subjective experience that accompanies the earlier stages of physical dissolution. For example, the first stage may be experienced as being like a television reception going blurry, or the mirage effect you see when driving along the road during a very hot summer. This may be accompanied by a strong feeling of sinking, and the person may ask to be propped up as they feel they are being drawn downwards, or are under pressure from a heavy weight. The second stage is like being in a room filled with smoke, and a person may feel extremely thirsty, as though everything inside them is drying up. They may feel suffocated, and irritated by the smoke-like appearances, and ask for water. Those who care for the dying may be familiar with reported experiences like these—for example, comments about how there must be a fire somewhere. The third stage appears like sparks from a fire, or a swarm of fireflies. By the time we get to the fourth stage, the image of a single, flickering flame, physical death is almost complete.

A friend of mine who was the victim of a landmine blast told me about being airlifted to hospital soon after the explosion. Medics feared he may lose his life. He told me that as he lay on a stretcher in a helicopter, he had a very clear memory of a candle flame gusting in the wind. He knew that if the flame blew out, he would die. He tried his best to will it to keep burning.

Whether or not our pets experience these exact same subjective experiences, we don't know. What we do know is that, at the end of stage four, when physical dissolution is complete, whether we are cat, dog or human, we are defined as dead in Western terms. Our hearts have stopped beating. Our brain is no longer functioning. We are now, medically speaking, a corpse.

From a Buddhist perspective, however, while physical dissolution has occurred, the four stages of mental dissolution are still to happen. The formless continuum of clarity and cognition remains in our body, experiencing increasingly subtle levels of consciousness—a process that can take from a few moments to much longer, until we arrive at the stage known as the clear light of death.

From the outside, it may seem that nothing is happening. The person, or our beloved pet, has died. Minutes may have passed. The main event appears to be over.

For the being who is moving on from this lifetime, however, mental dissolution leads to the *most* important time of all. The thoughts, feelings and sensations that arise at this time have the capability not only to shape our experience of reality for that particular moment. When accompanied by the wish for embodiment, they propel us into an intermediary, bardo form. And from there, to a whole new lifetime of this reality.

Used to experiencing ourselves as flesh and blood beings, whatever species we belong to, when encountering our most subtle mental states, we may have a sense of personal annihilation. Where am 'I'? What's happened to 'me'? I want to 'be'! This grasping for a self, together with whatever other thoughts may be arising in our mind, is what propels us into the bardo state—the one that exists between the lifetime that has just ended, and the one that is to come.

This is why it is all-important to ensure that our loved ones, animal or human, die in the most peaceful way possible, and that they are given the time they need to make the transition before we tamper with their bodies. Their very subtle minds may be present for much longer than we think.

THROUGH THE BARDO STATE TO REBIRTH

The bardo state may be likened to a dream. In dreams we can see, taste, touch and do everything we can in normal wakefulness, even though we are not doing so physically. Our feelings are often greatly heightened. In fact, what we experience when dreaming may be very much more vivid and dramatic than anything that happens to us when awake. And all that we experience, positive or negative, is a projection of our mind.

In the bardo state we take the subtle form of the being we will next be born as—human or animal—and we are constantly seeking the opportunity for rebirth. At this time nothing is certain. The karma that links us to potential parents may be strong, but is conception possible? What about others who have karmic links to those same beings?

It is said that in the bardo state, we only need to think about a place, and we are there, much like in a lucid dream. If we think about our previous home, we are present. In some Buddhist cultures, for seven weeks after the death of a person, their belongings are left ready for use and their place at the dining table is set, so that if they were to observe what is happening as bardo beings, they would not feel forgotten or excluded. For the sake of leaving out a few familiar food bowls, this is useful advice for pet lovers too.

The minds of bardo beings can also be influenced by those with whom they have recently had close karmic bonds. Loved ones can practise generosity or make donations of various kinds, offering the virtue for the benefit of those who have passed on, thereby influencing what happens to their mind—and their future—in the bardo state. This is another key instruction for pet lovers.

Our time in bardo can last from just moments up to seven weeks. We may find rebirth very easily, or it could take a while. Each week, on the anniversary of the day of our death, the subtle form of the bardo being undergoes a form of mini-death, or reboot, and the being may arise with a different subtle form. So, the possibility of our rebirth may change from, say, a cat to a human, or vice versa. This is highly significant. Depending on what throwing karma or finishing karma arises, the kind of reality we may broadly experience, potentially for many decades, can be affected by what happens at this critical time. In the bardo state, as in life, all depends on the combination of what is arising in our mind, what influences we are experiencing and what possibilities are available to us.

By the 49th day after death, every bardo being will definitely have found an opportunity for rebirth. Having entered a fertilised egg, the framework for our experience of reality for another lifetime is set.

PUTTING OUR PETS FIRST

Having provided a brief overview of the death process, what are the main implications for us when taking care of our dying pet?

First and foremost is the need to emphasise that what we are going through and what our pet is going through are two entirely separate experiences. This may seem obvious, but there's often a very real risk of confusing our own thoughts and feelings for those of our pet.

Being told that our pet is dying is traumatic, even if the kindly intended euphemisms used by vets don't always express what's happening quite so bluntly. It's natural to feel upset at the prospect of losing our dearly loved friend, or anxious that they may be in pain.

But if we accept that our pet really does have consciousness, and that their mind will move on from this experience to another, then we recognise that our pets' thoughts and feelings must come first. We will still be living in a few weeks or months, but they won't. We have a limited period in which to be a positive influence—one that may have a huge impact on our pet's future experience. During that time they certainly won't benefit from being looked after by a neurotic, weepy human. To whatever extent they may be aware that they will soon pass on, their state of mind is best helped if we remain as supportive, calm and loving as possible. Our focus must be not on our own emotions, but on our pets' wellbeing.

BrightHaven is a holistic animal sanctuary, hospice, rescue and education centre in Santa Rosa, California, offering a home to hundreds of older pets, including those who are sick and disabled. Over the years, Gail and Richard Pope, who established BrightHaven, have begun to educate pet lovers—through books, workshops and online programs—on how best to support pets through their time of transition.

Their booklet, 'Soar, My Butterfly: The Animal Dying Experience' provides unique information on what to expect, in terms of behavioural and physical changes a few months before death, a few weeks before death, and in the immediate approach and experience of the death process. It is an invaluable resource.

One to three months before death, our pets may withdraw, spending more time alone, sleeping for longer or being more affectionate. In the immediate weeks before death they may also sometimes be disorientated or agitated.

Managing a pet's pain should be our priority as this life draws to a close. Because pets can't speak or overtly show they are in pain, we need to observe them closely and also heed our intuition. If our pet starts behaving in an uncharacteristic manner—for example, holding themselves differently or reeling away from us for no apparent reason— we need to visit the vet urgently. We also need to be aware of the wide range of available holistic treatments that can assist in palliative care.

Apart from pain management and helping ensure our pets are physically comfortable during this time, the best assistance we can give our pet is to spend time meditating with them, and showing our love and affection as we recite mantras. Their association of mantras and meditation with positive mental experiences is an incredibly powerful and positive one. If we have already established this in everyday life, we have helped create a habit, a norm, of inestimable benefit to their future wellbeing.

Gail Pope of BrightHaven talks about the need to 'reverse' the grieving process, by which she means that instead of thinking and talking about our shared experiences with our animal companions *after* they have died, we should do so in their final days, when we have accepted that their death is inevitable. Now is the moment to tell them how much we love them, and how much we will miss their physical presence. This is the time to relive memories, to laugh and to cry; as we care for our beloved friend during their final time on earth, we are creating a bond that will never be forgotten.

Says Gail:

> We know that animals come to us to teach us life lessons and we've learned that many of these lessons become clearly apparent in their final days. By savouring death in all its wisdom, we can learn so much about living. It is in the last moments of life that small miracles can happen, thereby changing lives forever. A paw raised to your cheek by one who has not moved for days; a lick of your hand from one who appears to have faded from

the physical world; these are sacred vignettes that illuminate the truly important aspects of living life well, all the way to its end.

EUTHANASIA

As we approach the time of transition, euthanasia is a subject that may arise. From the Greek term for 'good death', the original purpose of euthanasia is to spare beings needless pain, especially once death becomes a certainty.

It is probably fair to say that euthanasia is no longer the way that a small minority of pets die. It has moved firmly mainstream. It is now quite common to hear both pet lovers and vets talk not so much about 'if' a pet may need to be put to sleep as 'when'.

This is not an approach that Buddhism encourages.

When I was mulling over the idea of this book, one of my first thoughts was: 'I'm going to have to deal with euthanasia and there will be people who don't like the Buddhist view on this.' I also felt a certain dissonance given that during the course of my life I have chosen to euthanise several of my own pets.

Let's begin at a starting point most of us would agree with: euthanasia should never be used as a way of getting rid of unwanted pets. We've all heard stories of perfectly healthy, if sometimes elderly, pets being put down because of changes in the family, or owners who simply couldn't be bothered to take care of them, or even try to find them new homes.

Things become more complicated when we know our pet is suffering and the vet has told us, categorically, that they are dying and suggested the best option is to put them to sleep.

A friend of mine, Hazel, found herself in exactly this situation with a dog who had become seriously ill and hadn't had a drink of water for three days. After returning home from that harrowing news at the vet, instead of going to bed as usual, that night she chose to sleep on the floor next to her beloved companion. In her heart she tried to send out the message to her dog: 'Whatever you want, I'm here for you. Please tell me. I'm listening.'

In the middle of the night, she felt her dog stir before getting up, making her way to the water bowl, and having a long drink. This was a major breakthrough given the dog's previous behaviour. Hazel had the strong sense that her dog wasn't ready to go. The following morning, she took her to a naturopath who provided a range of holistic therapies. In the days that followed, the dog responded to the treatment, before returning to near normal health. All that happened over a year ago and her dog is still thriving, active and enjoying life.

Readers have sent me many other stories of pets who were due to be euthanised, even to the point of visits to the vet for the final procedure, when they have had the feeling 'my pet isn't ready to go'. Being open to intuition, willing to listen to the still, small voice, has been the difference between proceeding down a course from which there is no return, and taking a different course, allowing their pets more precious months, even years, of life.

Can we always be really sure that death is certain, even when the vet tells us that it is? Vets are certainly knowledgeable, and often highly experienced, compassionate and wise. But they are not clairvoyant. Surprise recoveries are possible, as are unexpected rallies. When we euthanise a pet, we are stopping nature in its tracks, halting any possibility that our pet may, in fact, have more quality time to live.

We also need to be open about the awkward question: how much am I really doing this for my pet, and how much for me? If my pet is free from pain, am I really doing this to help them avoid suffering, or so that I don't have to deal with the pain of watching my loved one dying? Who am I trying to protect from trauma—my pet, or myself?

Animal hospice is defined as 'care for animals, focused on the patient's and family's needs; on living life as fully as possible until the time of death—with or without intervention; and on attaining a degree of preparation for death'.[3] A growing number of animal hospice practitioners advocate for natural death to be the chosen route, with euthanasia only to be considered in situations where pain control, daily care, comfort or funding cannot be maintained. At BrightHaven, for example, the last euthanasia was 185 deaths ago. But in the words of Gail Pope: 'I have cared for more than 600 animals at the end of their lives since 1990 and they have taught me more than I can ever say about life and love and the circle of life . . . I have learned that there is no greater gift in life than to be present during the hospice time as well as at the end of this beautiful journey, to share love with another, and most especially to do so with courage and grace.'

Gail says that, over and over again, animals continue to show us not to project our own ideas onto what is, or may be, happening to them. We cannot predict death and, frequently, just as death is nigh, the animal recovers for a day, a week, months or longer.

These are all good lessons to simply accept what is, to live in and for the moment, to offer whatever palliative support is available and to meditate for the highest good of our pet—whether that means peaceful death, or a recovery to continued life.

The reason that Buddhist teachers oppose euthanasia also has to do with the karmic implications for our pet. If we accept the death process outlined earlier, it's clear to see that how we transition from this lifetime to the next is subject to many variables—our state of mind and the karma that arises being the main ones. Natural dying better enables our pet to come to terms with what is happening and mentally prepare for it.

Animals know when death is happening and their behaviour may change, sometimes quite dramatically. I have received stories from readers telling me how pets have approached a dying human with a perhaps uncharacteristic and explicit expression of compassion and affection. For example, one person's small dog, who never ventured up to her bedroom, as the staircase was of the open variety and the dog risked a serious fall, made his ascent for the first—and only—time to be with her on the night that turned out to be her last.

It is also the case that cats and dogs will often remain close to one another, in some cases forming a circle around a dying member of the pride of their family for hours, days or even weeks before their death. 'Anam Cara' is a Celtic phrase for 'soul friend' and Gail Pope uses it as a fitting title for the death midwife who is present at this end-of-life transition, in the same way that the birth midwife seeks to ease the start-of-life transition. Sometimes an animal will remain after death for a long period of time, and other animals may come to pay their respects. This is as true of animals in the wild as of our pets: a very well-watched YouTube video shows how elephants travelled for many kilometres to pay their final respects after 'elephant whisperer' Lawrence Anthony died in Southern Africa. The simple truth may be that our pets understand the death process on a level we humans seem to have forgotten. Abruptly terminating that process may be something for which they are unprepared.

What is the karmic impact of our pet dying prematurely—from their side—without understanding the enormity of what's happening? How will they cope with an abrupt physical and mental dissolution without notice? We are hardly helping them make the best of this critical transition.

There are further implications to do with suffering. If it is our pet's karma to experience pain, we can help with pain management. But what if we cut short that experience through euthanasia? Instead of pain mitigated by pain-killers, perhaps our loved one will have to experience it without? Surely that's the last thing we would wish on them? What will a mind in pain experience in the bardo and beyond?

Lamas warn us that we have no idea about the karmic implications of what we do, when we decide on euthanasia. Even if we are motivated by the very best of intentions, we are entirely ignorant of the karmic repercussions. It is very much better if we can help our pet transition via the natural death process.

Given the traditional Buddhist view of euthanasia, I have never heard lamas discuss the process itself. My personal experience, however, is that not all euthanasia is the same. In fact, the options available could not be more starkly different. The fully conscious cat on the table of the vet clinic, amid the bright lights and heightened tensions, having their paw shaved and a needle inserted into a vein, is a very different state of affairs from the sedated cat lying in a favourite spot at home, surrounded by loved ones when the procedure occurs.

The pressures of time and money are such that many vets may offer euthanasia only at their clinic. In such circumstances there is little opportunity for a sedative to be administered, or for a loving and meaningful goodbye. This seems a coldly sterile, dislocated and inappropriate final act by which to end one of the most intimate and precious relationships of our lives. And from our pet's perspective, certainly not the one they would wish.

Some vets will offer a euthanasia service at home; there are mobile vets who offer exactly this. They offer the chance to sedate a pet with a painless injection, and will leave the room, offering us the opportunity to be with our pet in a familiar environment, and to take our time saying our goodbyes, whispering mantras and communicating our gratitude and love, heart to heart. By the time we are ready, our pet is sedated and the final act of euthanasia can be performed in a gentler way.

WHAT TO DO AROUND THE TIME OF DEATH?

How can we be of greatest benefit to our pet at the time of their death?

Keeping them pain-free and comfortable: Focusing on their spiritual needs is our most important priority. This transition is all about them. We can do our best to ensure they are in as little pain, and are as physically comfortable, as possible. We can also try to rein in our own emotions, creating a safe, loving atmosphere and the most peaceful environment we can.

Meditating for a calm transition: Enabling our pet to make their transition in a calm state of mind is one of the greatest services we can offer them. If you are a Buddhist, and have formed the habit of repeating Chenrezig mantras in the presence of your pet (*Om mani padme hum*), now is a very good time to continue the practice.

Alternatively, you may wish to practise the taking and giving meditation provided in the previous chapter or simply offer your compassionate presence. You should not underestimate the power of what you are doing at this critical time in your pet's transition.

Being supportive during the vital period after death: Remember that even after the physical death of your pet, their subtle mind may still be present in their body. Don't move them. Instead, recognise that the mind of your pet is still in a most vital part of transition and that because of your relationship, you can exert an extremely beneficial influence as they enter the bardo state.

Continuing to be present for your pet, for at least an hour or two after the time of death, is most useful. If, for some reason, you can no longer be physically present with them, then continuing to meditate on their behalf afterwards, and dedicating whatever merit from your practice for their wellbeing, can be of immeasurable benefit.

At BrightHaven, pets are given a full three days for their life energy to depart, during which they are prepared in a beautiful bed or basket, surrounded by favourite toys, as well as candles, flowers and greenery. A traditional ceremonial Tibetan Buddhist prayer scarf completes the scene along with any other mementos of the life lived. During this time, friends, family and volunteers visit to pay their respects, meditate, offer prayers and bid the loved one farewell for one last time.

HOW TO BE OF SERVICE IN THE SEVEN WEEKS AFTER DEATH

In the immediate aftermath of our pet's death we may have a feeling of release, relief, of shifting energy, perhaps even of freedom as our pet moves on from an aged or sick body. Or we may simply be bereft at the loss of our beloved companion. Whatever our emotions, what's important is to recognise that while life has changed for us, it has changed in an even more dramatic and potentially challenging way for our pet, and it is within our power to continue to help them.

MEDITATING AND MANTRAS ON THEIR BEHALF

In the bardo state, your pet may still have some awareness of you, and perhaps other family members, irrespective of where you are physically. They can still be positively influenced by your practice of meditation and mantra recitation, particularly if you dedicate any virtue arising from the practice for their benefit. For seven weeks after the passing of your pet, you are still able to help them, and should do so to whatever extent you are able. As Tulku Thondup says in his book, *Peaceful Death, Joyful Rebirth*, 'Beings in the bardo, in particular, are very receptive to meditation and prayers, as they live in a world of thought.'[4] He also suggests: 'Meditation is a more powerful way to help these beings than our usual discursive thoughts and feelings because it comes from a deeper, more peaceful level in our mind.'[5]

While meditation is powerful, it needn't be the only time we can be of service. You don't have to wait until you are sitting on your meditation cushion, in a quiet room, to recite mantras. You can do so, under your breath, as you sit in the car, go to the gym, take a walk and in everyday life. Even in a room full of people, you can recite mantras mentally, without needing to move your lips.

Given that 'mini-death' is experienced by a being in bardo every seven days, this is a particularly vital time to focus your attention and practice on your loved one—by the way, this applies to all beings, human and animal. You may wish to mark a calendar with the day that your companion died, and on the weekly anniversary of that day, for seven weeks, redouble your meditation or recitation activities for their benefit. This is particularly the case on Day 49, which you may regard as your last chance to be of support to the one who has passed, before they move on into their next life—and you move on with yours.

A suggested dedication is as follows:

By this practice of the meditation/virtue/generosity
May NAME OF PET, and all beings, quickly enjoy higher rebirth.
Meet the perfect teacher, and attain enlightenment,
For the benefit of all beings without exception.

MAKING OFFERINGS ON THEIR BEHALF

Apart from meditation and Dharma practice, Buddhism encourages us to practise generosity, to whatever extent we are able, and dedicate the virtue to the benefit of the being in bardo state. You don't have to be rich to be generous. A poignant photograph I saw on social media showed a poor woman making flat bread to feed her child on a gas stove, at the side of a dusty road. In the image she is shown breaking off a small piece to feed a nearby bird.

You may feed ducks, birds or other animals. You may send a donation, or a series of donations to wildlife or other charities. You may drop a few coins in a charity collector's tin. When you do so, recollect your pet, and your bodhichitta motivation, and dedicate the virtue for their benefit.

Once again, it is useful to time this on the daily anniversary of your pet's passing, when their bardo state is in possible transition, and your positive influence can have greatest impact.

KEEPING THE PET BOWLS OUT

At any time in the bardo, our pets' minds may turn to their old home, and they may perceive what is happening there. To avoid creating possible distress for them, it's best to keep the landmarks of their old life unchanged, as though they may come back to us at any moment.

It is kind to keep your pet's feeding bowls, favourite rugs or basket in the usual place, as much as you are able. If the sight of these now unused items upsets you, use this as a prompt to say some mantras, verbally or mentally, and dedicate them for the benefit of your pet. Think of them as prompts to help keep the focus of your mind on the welfare of your pet, as they move through the bardo. And remember: this is all about them.

THE PRACTICAL AND SPIRITUAL BENEFITS OF BUDDHIST PRACTICES

This approach to helping our pets through the death process and the bardo stage has a number of profound benefits. Having outlined the process, and recommended actions you can take, the focus of this chapter has been on how we can best help our animal companions through the most important transition of their lives.

From a Buddhist perspective, there is no greater gift we can offer our pet than to do whatever we can to help them maintain a peaceful state of mind during the death process, knowing that they are surrounded by love and positivity, and by helping direct their journey through the bardo using the power of mantra, meditation and other offerings. Of course we live in a messy world, where things seldom go exactly as we would like. But it is useful to know what we are setting out to achieve.

What if you have doubts about the Buddhist presentation of death, bardo and rebirth? If you are unfamiliar with some of these concepts, it is understandable that, at the very least, you need time to reflect on them.

It's important always to remember that you don't have to believe anything. All you need is an open mind. Unless you are convinced by a different model of the death process, here, at least, is something useful that you can work with. What's more, the advantages of the practices outlined go well beyond benefiting our pets alone.

One of the most debilitating aspects of losing a loved one is the way that our thoughts turn to ourselves. How upset *I* am to lose this beautiful being. How bereft and lonely *I* am that they are gone. How *my* relationship with them was irreplaceable. The common element in all these understandable, natural but painful thoughts is 'me'.

By using mental habits and practices that have our pet as the focus of our thoughts, we shift our focus. When we are thinking about the wellbeing of someone else, we are, by necessity, not thinking about ourselves. And that pragmatic shift of focus means that we suffer less.

'Suffer' comes from a Latin root meaning 'to bear' or 'to carry'. When we carry around our grief, by continually thinking about our own personal loss, we extend and magnify our pain. But if we can replace those thoughts with different, other-centric thoughts, not only are we better able to help our pet, we will also recover our own peace of mind faster and easier.

A further benefit of the Buddhist approach to death is that the seven-week bardo period gives us a fixed period of time during which to focus our energies on the mind stream of our departed pet. By the 49th day, our companion will definitely have moved on. They will have a new life, a new reality. And that gives us permission to move on with our own lives too.

Of course it's natural to hearken back to the way things were. To wish for one more cuddle. One more walk through the woods. One more evening of contentment at the fireside. It's entirely normal for us to wish this and to hold onto cherished memories.

But by Day 49, the mind of our companion, that formless continuum of clarity and cognition, is experiencing a different reality—and so are we. We are richer for having known them, and wiser for having accompanied them through the most important transition of their lives.

It is time for both of us to embark on adventures new.

THE DEATH PROCESS IN BUDDHISM: WHERE DOES IT COME FROM?

Where does Buddhism's very detailed outline of the death process come from, and why should we give it any credence?

One of the great advantages of being part of a living tradition is that we not only have access to documented outlines, which have been composed, debated and refined over millennia, we also live alongside an unbroken chain of yogis, or meditation masters, who have devoted themselves to the exploration of consciousness.

Most of us would be doing extremely well to achieve level five of the established nine levels of meditative concentration. Meditation masters have not only achieved level nine—calm abiding—they have also explored non-conceptual states in which increasingly subtle levels of consciousness can be experienced directly. These increasingly subtle levels of consciousness are what we will all go through when we die.

Can advanced yogis undergo a similitude of physical death right up to the experience of clear light as part of their meditation? Yes. And many other interesting things besides. It is the shared experience of these yogis that provides the basis of our understanding of the death process. It is also their ability to directly perceive the causality of karma from one lifetime to another, including the death process, that underpins our confidence in the traditional teachings.

For a detailed description of the death, bardo and rebirth, I recommend *Peaceful Death, Joyful Rebirth* by Tulku Thondup, a lucid treasury of inestimable value.

CHAPTER TEN

REBIRTH

Allen Wilson, from England, met Honey while on holiday
in Spain. 'It was like a bolt of electricity. I knew at that
moment, with absolute conviction, that this was Clairelle,
she had "come back"'!

OUR MUCH-LOVED PET HAS died. The seven-week bardo period has come to an end. We have done all we can to give our animal companion a peaceful death, and the best possible chances for the most favourable rebirth.

A number of questions may quite naturally arise: will I ever encounter my pet again? Better yet, will I do so in this lifetime? Is there a chance my beloved companion will come back to me in some shape or form?

REBIRTH AND REINCARNATION

Reincarnation is one of the concepts most closely associated with Buddhism, but in the West there is confusion about what the term actually means. There is a vague—and very much mistaken—view of Buddhism that after we die we decide where we want to be born next, and by some arcane process, this is precisely what happens.

As discussed in the previous chapter, it is not the acquired personality that dies and moves from one lifetime to another but, rather, subtle consciousness. And through the death, bardo and rebirth process, as through life, that subtle consciousness is propelled into different experiences of reality by cause and effect, or karma.

Some of the most important meditative training we undertake as Tibetan Buddhists is to prepare for the death process, to recognise the different stages and, to whatever extent we are able, manage the process. Our ultimate goal is to achieve liberation from the constant cycle of birth, ageing, death and rebirth and to achieve enlightenment, so that we can help all other beings to the same state. If we haven't evolved sufficiently for that, at least we wish to achieve human rebirth, and to come under the care of an enlightened teacher so that we may continue our journey.

For most of us, karma will drive what happens to us—hence the Buddhist wish to create as many positive causes for future positive effects as possible. But a very small proportion of people, whose minds are no longer propelled by karma, but by virtue, do have the capacity to direct their consciousness to future rebirths. They may choose to be reborn as a human or, indeed, any other being. We regard these people as bodhisattvas, enlightened beings.

Our birth, propelled by karma, is known as rebirth. Their birth, propelled by altruism, is reincarnation.

His Holiness the Dalai Lama is regarded by most Tibetan Buddhists as a bodhisattva, who has returned to be with us many times. There are countless other lamas, yogis and lay people who have attained enlightenment in the past, and who choose to return to live among us, and help us on the path to this day. I have no doubt, for example, that my own teacher Geshe Acharya Thubten Loden, who died several years ago, will soon be making his presence felt. He will almost certainly be nothing like the Geshe-la we knew. But as an extraordinary being, he will be more than capable of revealing who we once knew him to be.

WOULD WE RECOGNISE OUR RETURNED PET?

What does the rebirth versus reincarnation distinction say about encountering our pet again in this lifetime? Unless our animal companion was an undercover bodhisattva—improbable, although possible—they will not have the capacity to direct their mind to return to live with us.

We may also ask ourselves: would we really want them to? Yes, we may long to lie out on the veranda with them, enjoying a spring morning or a summer evening, but if we truly wish for their best possible future, wouldn't we rather they be reborn as a human being, with the motivation and opportunities to continue their spiritual journey? Is our motivation that they come back to us really for their benefit, or is it for our own?

A second, much bigger question is: would we be capable of recognising them? Given that it is not the ego, the acquired personality, that is reborn, how would we know whether the new being in our midst is the reborn version of our previous pet? Clairvoyance may be natural and effortless for highly realised beings, but what about us more ordinary people?

The reality is that not only are we unlikely to recognise a returned pet, we also have no idea about the past relationships we've had with the close family, friends and pets who currently surround us. We would probably be startled if we were to find out.

A traditional Buddhist story is sometimes quoted by lamas to illustrate exactly this point. It tells the tale of how Shariputra, a close disciple of Buddha, walked past what, to most people, looked like a scene of cosy domesticity. Because of his clairvoyance, however, Shariputra could see the backgrounds of the various participants, which put things in a rather different perspective.

The background goes like this: A young couple lived in the home of the husband's parents, and behind the home there was a lake in which the old father enjoyed fishing. They were a happy family and the old mother was proud of keeping a happy home. However, one day a visitor came and during his stay committed adultery with the young wife. Her husband found out, and in a rage, killed the man then and there. Shortly after, the young couple conceived a child who, due to his strong karmic connection and attachment to the wife, was the rebirth of her dead lover. As time went on, both of the ageing parents died. The mother, being strongly attached to the house, was reborn as the couple's pet dog. The father's love of fishing in the lake saw him come back as a fish.

One day the young husband went fishing and caught the fish that had been his father. His wife fried it and threw the bones to the dog. Cradling his baby on his lap, the man ate the fish while kicking away the dog.

Walking past, when Shariputra saw this scene he said:

He eats his father's flesh and kicks his mother.
He cradles the enemy he killed in his lap.
A wife gnaws her husband's bones.
Cyclic existence can be such a joke.[1]

Thinking about our own families, this is an insight that certainly gives pause for thought!

NEW LIVES AND CURIOUS ENCOUNTERS

Our pets may lack the ability to direct their minds to return to us in their next life, but what if the strength of their attachment to us, or our home—like the mother in the story just quoted—propels them in our direction? What exactly is the nature of our past relationships with our children, pets, partner and friends? The Buddhist view is that karma plays a key role. The beings with whom we share our lives are not here by accident.

Ginos, a cafe in Fremantle, Western Australia, is one of the best known landmarks on the main street, having been around since long before the concept of a cappuccino strip was even thought of. Founded by Gino Saccone, with his wife Rosa and daughter Laura, the owner was, in true Italian style, a constant presence in the cafe, sitting in a particular chair which gave him a good vantage point over the whole restaurant. After he died in 2001, a curious thing happened. A willie wagtail bird hopped into the cafe, made its way quite deliberately through the restaurant, and flew onto the back of Gino's chair. It remained there for quite some time.

Daughter Laura had no doubt what the visit signified. And it turned out to be no fleeting experience. In the months and years since then, the bird has become a daily visitor, always flying to the same chair. If Laura sits on the chair, it refuses to move. And when other staff have tried to shoo it away, it always returns. Quoted in the local paper, Laura said, 'I think the bird just wants me to know it's Dad. A lot of people don't believe in this stuff, but I do.'[2]

Asking readers via my blog if they had any sense of previous connections, I was inundated with stories. Many people said they had the strongest feelings, instincts or intuition about a variety of beings. I'd like to share a few of these in the readers' own words:

From a reader in the United Kingdom:

I lost my beloved cat Natasha at twelve years old from squamous cell cancer, which was underneath her tongue. I was afraid it would choke her and she would die alone and horribly when I was at work, so I had her put down while I held her. I was completely devastated and destroyed.

I adopted a new kitten six months later from a gal at work who had rescued a sack of kittens from a man who was about to throw it into a river and she was the last one left. I took her back to my cubicle where she hopped behind my corner phone and went to sleep. When I brought her home, she walked over to the pile of cat toys in the kittyland corner, rooted through it to the back and bottom of the pile and then walked to me with my Natasha's very favourite toy from kittenhood through her entire life. She dropped it at my feet, cocked her head and just looked at me … and I knew she had returned to me.

She also greeted me when I came home by rising up on her back paws and pushing her head into my outstretched palm, just like Natasha did every day. All I could think of was[,] when the Dalai Lama reincarnates, one of the tests is that he must pick out his belongings from a previous incarnation among a group of things and know that they were his.

The new kitten had facets of a new personality to go with the new form but I knew exactly who she was. She cleaved to me, staying with me for almost sixteen more years and I was grateful for every single day. I lost her again suddenly yet I know she waits for me and I will be with her again.

From Nici Ott in Perth:

My mother passed away, very quickly and unexpectedly, when I was 33 years old. The night before she became unwell and then ended up in a coma, we had a very lovely and peaceful—to us unbeknownst last—telephone conversation and we parted at total ease and with the words 'I love you'. The next day my world crumbled.

About a year later, [as] I was still a very keen scuba diver at that time, my husband and myself travelled to Tobago for a diving holiday. One day, we were luckily diving in fairly shallow water, our group of six divers got surrounded, rather herded, by a group of ten manta rays. They just floated around us, so calm and still so inquisitive. Especially one of them was extremely interested in myself, it came so close, literally stopped in front of me and gave me that long peaceful look. It felt like that amazing creature was looking deeply into my soul trying to comfort me, and I knew those eyes. They were my mum's eyes, and she was telling me, she loved me and all was good. She was in a happy place now, watching over me. I will be forever grateful for this moment in time.

From Rhea Baldino in Virginia, United States:

I've hardly ever told this story because part of it is just too horrible to tell (at least by me; throat won't cooperate!). But the last part is nothing short of extraordinary. This may be long because it covers several decades, and has two distinct parts.

Several decades ago, my husband and I adopted three kittens from a farm where we were boarding a horse. Two were long hair and one short (different fathers). One of the long hair ones turned out to be one of the great treasures of my life; I named her RumDum after one of Jackie Gleason's characters on TV. Over the years, she became one of my best all-time soul mates.

When RumDum was around eighteen, she was pretty much deaf, didn't respond to sound, only touch, but was still her usual purring, loving self otherwise. I still let her out some and she just padded around the base of our house. But one day when I went out to bring her back in, I couldn't find her. I looked and looked and called and called (although that wouldn't have done any good since she couldn't hear anymore).

I was devastated and thought she must have gotten herself lost outside and become prey to something.

A couple [of] years later, I encountered a lady who lived about half a mile down our road and was telling her about this. She said she remembered the cat and had found her in her yard.

Not knowing who she belonged to, she took her to the county pound. (I do so wish she had asked around the neighbourhood!)

I never thought RumDum could get that far down the road at her age, for me to go to the pound. It didn't have a very good reputation and I never imagined how she would get there. At that time, they kept animals for five days and then euthanized them in a gas chamber along with however many others would fit in at the same time. (As I said, too horrible to contemplate.)

Since then, this has been one of three or four memories in my life that Eckhart Tolle refers to as your 'pain body'. I can't think of it without feeling the pain again; it's just a deep seated, permanent part of me.

Cut to several decades later, about thirteen years ago now. The shelter grew and modernized and were more adoption oriented and I started walking dogs there. They still weren't doing much for cats, but eventually initiated a practice of allowing moms with underage kittens to go out to foster care till the kittens were old enough to be adopted. I got the first mom and litter to become available!

The lady there said they had two moms with babies and did I want to pick out which family I wanted. I said no, I didn't want to do that, would she please make the choice for me. She did.

When I got home and saw them up close, I was dumbfounded at what I saw. One of the kittens was just about an exact replica of RumDum who was euthanized there in the gas chamber years earlier. I got out pictures and compared them—sure enough, almost exact look-alikes as kittens! And even more astounding, this new baby had the same instant purr, attentiveness, personality, and temperament of the first one! There was no way she was going back to the shelter for adoption!

I have called her my Buddha kitty ever since then, thirteen years ago. Her name is Rumble because of her purr and partly named after RumDum. I call her my 'BuddhaPuss', or just Bump for short.

I don't know whether there really is reincarnation or not, although I do believe in the universal or cosmic consciousness and think I can feel it in my cats too, especially some who seem to exude it more than others.

So this whole story is either an extraordinary coincidence or it's a remarkably obvious case of reincarnation—as though RumDum finally managed to come back to me from the shelter. I'd like to believe it's the latter!

From a reader in Oregon, United States:

At around two years of age, our second son, Brian, used to wander away from the house. This was over fifty years ago and we lived in a semi-rural place. Brian spent most of his time with his big brother, and parents were more relaxed about their children in those days.

We lived next to a field where elderly neighbors kept a horse. Brian used to crawl between the fence posts into the field. The old couple, Cecil and Emily, seemed nice, but we didn't know them well. They kept to themselves. As well as the horse, they had a dog, chickens and ducks.

One afternoon, Brian came into the house with a note in his shirt pocket. He had been to visit the neighbors, and Cecil had written saying he was worried something might happen with the horse. I visited them that same afternoon. Cecil told me the horse had never been aggressive, but he wasn't used to children. It turned out that Brian had been to visit Cecil and Emily several times that we hadn't known about. Emily laughed when she described how eager Brian was to follow Cecil around as he did his chores, and how he would sit at his feet watching closely as he carved blocks of wood by hand, which was his hobby.

We warned Brian about the field and the horse. We didn't want to put him off horses, so we said it was better to wait till he was bigger before he goes into the field. We thought it was just a phase that would wear off.

The warning seemed to work for a while. Then one day we couldn't find him. My wife went over to Cecil and Emily's and sure enough he was there. It turned out that Brian had arrived at a time when the couple had some workmen in to dig the ground near their rockery where they had a home-made waterfall. One of the pipes was leaking and needed to be replaced. It was too much for Cecil to do, but he was overseeing the workmen. Brian had wanted to be with him, but my wife arrived to find Emily holding him to her, a short distance away. She whispered to my wife that, a couple of years before, Cecil had buried their deceased dog in that area. They weren't sure what would be left of its remains, but didn't want Brian to see whatever was left.

My wife took Brian's hand, and was about to lead him home, when he broke away from her suddenly and rushed over to where they were digging. On the pile of soil they had unearthed, was some mud-smeared object. He grabbed it and started shouting what sounded like 'My!' or 'Maya!' over and over. He was very excited. My wife hurried over to get him. She noticed the strange look that came over Emily. She thought Emily was fearful that Brian might see something horrible.

Cecil helped guide Brian away from the dig. Bending to look at the mud-smeared object Brian was holding, he said that it looked like a small doll that had once been in the family. Brian had it firmly in his clutches. Cecil said he could keep it. My wife didn't want to make a big thing of it and brought Brian home. In the laundry tub, she persuaded him to let her wash the very battered doll, which she did in hot, disinfected water.

At the time, we didn't think too much about what happened. We were more worried about Brian's continued visits and him being kicked by the horse. For a few weeks, Brian treasured what had once been a doll, but was now more just like a stick with some tufts of fur on it. But when Christmas came, he replaced it with a new favorite toy.

One other thing to mention is that we were once out in the local diner, and who should step in but Emily and Cecil and their grown-up daughter, Carol. We had finished our meal and were about to leave, but for a few minutes we all sat together in the same booth. Brian, who was quite shy of strangers at that stage, immediately took to Carol and made his way to her. We commented on how unusual it was. Within minutes he was sitting on Carol's lap as she made a big fuss of him.

Cecil died about five years after this. My wife and I went to the funeral. It was a small gathering and we were invited back to their home afterwards. We got to meet Cecil and Emily's other daughter and son and also saw Carol again.

At some point, Carol was talking to my wife and me. She asked us a lot of questions about Brian—when was his birthday, did he like water, detailed stuff like that. She also asked us if we believed in reincarnation. My wife told her that she did. I hadn't made up my mind. She said she didn't want to shock us with what she was about to say, but when she was much younger, her parents had taken her to the local dogs' home, where she'd picked out a puppy. She named him Duke, because he had a regal appearance. She doted on Duke, and so did her parents. When she left home for college, Duke became more her father's dog. He would follow Cecil everywhere as he did his household chores and loved sitting at his feet when he did his wood carving.

After college, Carol had gone travelling. She had sent a doll home from her time in Mexico. Its name was Maya, and it had somehow become Duke's favorite toy. Cecil had thought Duke could smell her on the doll. When Duke died, Cecil had buried him near the rockery. Because Maya had been his favorite toy, he had buried the doll right beside him.

I am sorry there are no big fireworks in this story. But I have always asked myself: why did Brian never 'wander' to the other neighbors, even though they had children? Why did he get so excited about the thing that was dug up which would have been of no interest to most two year olds? And even know Maya's name?

We spoke to Brian about the whole thing, in his teens. He clearly remembered finding Maya as a young boy—the only memory he had from that very young age. And he always had a soft spot for Carol and Emily. Even when Emily was very elderly, he would go visit her, which was unusual for a teenage boy. He remembered nothing else about a time before being Brian. There is an obvious explanation for all this, but I like to let people come to their own conclusion.

HUMANS RETURNING AS PETS?

As well as pets returning to people who felt the strongest of bonds for them, I have also received a number of stories from readers who had the strongest feeling that their pets were the new manifestations of family members with whom they'd had the strongest of bonds.

From Rebecca Hartman in Pennsylvania, United States:

I had a difficult start in life and it was left mainly to my grand-mother, Johanna Jentsch, to bring me up. 'Jo', as she was known to friends, was tall, elegant and beautiful, and often sang to me in her sweet, melodic voice. She had something of an air of entitlement, an air of superiority. She also had terrible allergies, often clearing her throat or blowing her nose.

Jo had the most gentle manner of anyone I have ever met. She detested conflict of any kind. She always sought to diffuse all tense emotions immediately. She was not like anyone else in my family.

Jo was a very spiritual woman in practice and in heritage. She had been married to a Lutheran minister, Hans, who was one of the four great loves of her life, along with Pixie the Siamese cat, myself ('Becky/her princess') and Jesus.

I lost my grandmother when she was 93 years of age. I was with her when she passed, and made sure to tell her how much I loved her, how grateful I was to her, and how it was OK to go.

After she died I started to discuss with my then husband how very upset I was and how I was worried that I wouldn't graduate from graduate school on time. Finally the coroner came. He asked us to step out. I had not cried yet at that point. I felt too numb. Then the coroner walked past us with my grandmother in a black body bag. I began to sob very, very loudly. I believe this sealed my grandmother's resolve to come back again to watch over me.

I found my grandmother again a couple of years after her passing, in not the most reputable pet shop, adjacent to a highway. I had decided to stop, on a whim, in an effort to cheer myself up. I was so deeply depressed that I could barely function at the time. Alone in a little cage was a tiny, ugly, cross eyed, blue point Siamese kitten, sneezing her little heart out. Price reduced to $200, possibly because she was sick and possibly because she was cross eyed. There was something about her. I felt bad for her. Plus the price was good. The owner handed me her pedigree papers. I could not believe the name of the cattery this little kitten I had just bought came from! 'Jo's Siamese'!!

That was seven years ago. I have many other cats. I have three other Siamese cats in fact. None are like Johanna. I do not doubt for one second that Johanna is my grandmother. She is the only cat who sleeps on my pillow, by my side when I am home, or directly on my chest every single day all day. If I begin to become upset or raise my voice Johanna reacts instantly to calm me down. Her typical intervention is a series of very specific meows or very gentle touches to my cheek with her paw. If someone else raises their voice she will run to them and give them her specific meows. She often gives me the most long, soulful stares when she's on my chest. She is also very intelligent, always clearing her throat, more entitled than any cat I've ever encountered (I have eleven), incredibly sweet and gentle, thin, beautiful, sophisticated, and carries herself with an air of superiority and grace that I have seen in no other cat and definitely in only one other person.

Interestingly, I received a number of emails from people who felt that a child who had been aborted had returned to them in a different form.

One of the most intriguing accounts comes from Allen Wilson in Buckinghamshire, England:

Clairelle died at the age of eight weeks from conception. Her mother—my then fiancée—aborted her. Like many people I had liberal views on abortion, but suddenly when it was my child those views went straight out the window. As a lawyer, I thought of trying an injunction to stop her, but it wouldn't have worked and would only have made things worse. The relationship ended there and then. Of course I didn't know the sex of the aborted child nor did I have any idea that I still had a living child afterwards: to think that would have been ridiculous, so I had assumed that was that.

Except it wasn't.

Five or six years later, I became interested in mediumship, Buddhism and parapsychology for reasons quite unconnected with the abortion, although the experience had been a shattering one. I started to fantasise about having a five- or six-year-old daughter, blonde and beautiful, alive and healthy. I have no other children. In the course of my research, I came across quite a few mediums, some of them the real deal with real ability. One or two amazingly recounted the whole experience to me, including places, names, even adding that there was a small blonde girl standing by me, trying to talk. Of course I saw and heard nothing, but was left wondering about the girl I came to name Clairelle, who felt utterly alone and said she wanted to find a way to be with me physically. This seemed unlikely as my partner and I were both around 50.

The years passed and my partner and I rented a villa in Mallorca. On arrival, we were met by a tortoiseshell cat, who made a beeline for me and was in obvious need of food and a home. Realising this, we bought her lots of food and offered her our temporary home to live in, sheltering her from one of the locals who hated cats and would shoot them as vermin. I named her Honey.

It was becoming hard to imagine how I would be able to leave her when the holiday ended. Then one day, as I sat by the pool, with Honey on the sun lounger with me, she suddenly squeaked and looked straight at me and it was like a bolt of electricity. I knew at that moment, with absolute conviction that this was Clairelle, she had 'come back'! Honey knew it too. Of course, Clairelle is not a cat, but instead some of her energy is in Honey, who is a willing participant. Of course Honey is her own cat. Suddenly everything made blindingly clear sense. The promise to return, the series of so called coincidences leading to my meeting Honey in the first place, the extraordinary attraction of Honey to me and me to Honey.

Now there was no choice. Honey had to come back to the UK. She spent six months in quarantine but when her sentence was over—February 2011—she came home. Aged about ten or eleven now, she is outside in the cool English spring sunshine as I type this. I have learned what it is to give and receive unconditional love from Honey, to feel the love of my daughter whom I will have to wait a while longer to see, and to learn that far more things are possible than most of us ever even imagine.

REBIRTH AND THE WEST

These are only a few of the very many intriguing stories other people have shared with me. A couple of things strike me about them. The first is that the people involved would have had encounters with many different people and animals over the years: would they have been so struck by these particular encounters if they hadn't felt, in some way, qualitatively different?

Another point that recurs in these accounts is that the meetings often seem to be in some way spur of the moment, or unsought. Rhea Baldino had no intention of taking on a new cat, except on a foster basis; Allen Wilson was in Spain on holiday; the reader from England arrived at work to find a colleague needing to find homes for rescued kittens.

While it is unlikely that empirical evidence could be found to support animal rebirth stories, over the past few decades a fair amount of research has been done among humans. For readers interested in exploring this subject further, the work of the late Canadian psychiatrist, Dr Ian Stevenson, is worth studying. Stevenson and others have documented many cases where children reported being able to recall past lives. He found powerful corroborating evidence to support their stories, such as evidence from family members with details they couldn't otherwise have known.

While not on a mission to prove the case for rebirth, Stevenson concluded that, in light of what he'd found, it wasn't unreasonable to accept that some people are reborn. Other academics, such as Professor Robert Almeder, have gone further, to suggest that it is irrational *not* to accept it.[3]

Exactly why relatively few people are able to report on past lives remains a mystery. But as Professor Almeder notes, it is these outliers, these statistical anomalies, that are the interesting ones, worthy of further study.

While rebirth is an assumed norm in some Eastern cultures, it is a different matter in the West. There are powerful, vested interests eager to refute the idea, as well as those who seek its possible validation. But despite these, a surprising number of people actually support it.

A 2012 survey by Pew Forum found that 25 per cent of all Americans and 24 per cent of Christians believe in reincarnation.

Having had the privilege of a Tibetan Buddhist education as well as a Western one, there's no doubt in my own mind about which provides the more coherent and useful explanation of consciousness and its workings.

I am not clairvoyant, but I know advanced meditators who are, and they leave us in no doubt about the beings we share our lives with. Parents, children, humans or pets, they are beings with whom we have powerful, shared karma. Mostly, we have no idea what our past relationships have been. Our job, in this lifetime, is to be a force for good. To make the most positive impact we can on those we share our lives with. If necessary, to heal past wounds. To support them to live in a way that best propels them on their own journey to enlightenment. And when, as our own pathway unfolds, we come to recognise them again in a future life—how wonderful!

CHAPTER ELEVEN

ANIMALS AND NON-HARMING: A FEW WIDER QUESTIONS

Horace, the vervet monkey, was adopted by tabby cat Tiger Lily when he arrived at the Twala Trust Animal Sanctuary in Zimbabwe. Unlikely interspecies friendships illustrate how compassion is not a uniquely human quality.

THE FOCUS OF THIS book is on how we can best help our animal companions in their spiritual journey through this life and into their next experience of reality. Because we interact with other animals far less than our own pets, our opportunity to help them is also generally less.

All the same, as we have explored the nature of animal sentience, and how all conscious beings are just like ourselves in wishing for happiness and to avoid dissatisfaction, a number of questions may naturally have arisen. Questions like: how should I deal with insect pests like cockroaches? What about animal factory farming—does Buddhism suggest we should all go vegan? And what, if anything, can I do about ways I have, out of ignorance, not done the best for other beings in the past?

In this chapter I try to answer some of these questions, providing answers that, in some cases, may differ according to your level of engagement in Buddhism.

SHOULD I BECOME A VEGAN/VEGETARIAN?

From a Buddhist perspective, is it desirable to go vegan or vegetarian? In a word, yes. The Dalai Lama has often said that removing meat and animal products from our diet is a very positive step. Cattle, pigs, lambs and chickens are sentient beings like us. They wish for lives of freedom and safety. They feel terror and pain, just like we do. On what basis can we say that our wish to eat their flesh overrides the suffering they must endure through the barbaric practices of factory farming, culminating in the horror of an untimely, mechanised and pitiless death?

It does not take any time or money for us to stop harming animals in this way.

The litmus test of any behaviour is to ask: what would happen if every person in the world did this? If everyone became vegan, within a matter of weeks, the factory farming industry, responsible for the deaths of 3000 animals *every second*, would come to an abrupt halt. Agri-business would rapidly refocus on plant-based alternatives.

The meat versus vegan debate is not, however, completely black and white. Vast quantities of pesticides are used to kill insects on the crops and fruit trees whose produce is eaten by vegans and vegetarians. What's more, when land is first cleared, whether to grow maize or rear cattle, the natural habitat is destroyed and, along with it, countless sentient beings to whom it was home.

While being a vegetarian or vegan brings an end to the horror of the abattoir, it does not end the killing of conscious beings. There is something unthinkingly size-ist and/or species-ist about only caring for beings that weigh over 20 grams, or are attractively cute or possess demonstrably high IQs.

Is it better to kill one cow or a thousand insects? I have encountered a wide variety of perspectives on this subject. Suffice it to say—we are now dealing in shades of grey. The sobering reality is that in order for us to live, others die.

This is a subject I contemplate every time I set out for Dharma class along roads where, at certain times of the year, I regularly drive through clouds of insects, killing countless dozens. Should I stay at home, rather, and avoid the mass slaughter, but also potentially hold back my inner development, the end result of which is enlightenment for the benefit of all beings, including the bugs themselves?

Given that there are few easy answers, the advice of lamas is to strive for moderation. If giving up meat completely seems a step too far, at least try to cut down significantly on your meat intake. As Matthieu Ricard points out in his book, *A Plea for the Animals*, the reasons people typically give for eating meat have no moral value—for example, because we like the taste of it; because it's too hard to change our habit of eating it; because others in the family eat it; because humans were 'made' to eat meat; because we don't know what else to cook.

A visit to the local vegetarian shelves of the supermarket will reveal that there are plenty of delicious meat substitute choices available. As omnivores, humans thrive without meat. And there are signs that more people in developed countries are choosing to become 'flexitarian', opting increasingly for vegetarian meal options.

Rather than simplistic directives about what you should and should not eat, therefore, Tibetan Buddhism encourages us to be mindful about the impact of our food and other lifestyle choices. To avoid gratuitous waste and the unseen horror and death that it brings to untold, voiceless others, conveniently out of sight. To recollect and honour the sacrifice they have been forced to make every time we sit down to eat a meal or enjoy a drink. To get into the habit of reflecting along the following lines, as we begin to eat our meal:

'By nourishing my body, may I quickly achieve complete and perfect enlightenment for the benefit of all living beings, and may those who died, so that I could eat this food, quickly achieve complete and perfect enlightenment.'

HOW SHOULD I DEAL WITH ANIMAL PESTS LIKE APHIDS, COCKROACHES AND OTHERS?

Aphids just want to be happy too. The trouble is, their flourishing requires the destruction of our rosebuds, and herein lies our dilemma.

Buddhists strive to live by the ideal of non-harmfulness. Compassion is one of the central themes of the tradition. So, too, is wisdom. Often, we need to apply both in equal measure.

There are many ways to help avoid being troubled by unwanted animals. Some of these preventative measures are common sense, like not leaving food out in places where it will attract ants, or spraying rosebuds, and other 'at risk' plants, with essential oils, which act as a powerful aphid/insect repellent.

We may need to do online research to learn about longer term, sustainable and non-harmful ways to deter insects and other animals from bothering us. For example, there are certain plants like onions, garlic and other alliums that repel aphids. Birdbaths, birdhouses and planting other bird-friendly plants will encourage a more balanced ecosystem in our garden that will also prevent aphid infestation.

At the Tibetan Buddhist centre I attend, which is bordered by a national park, we have ended up having to remove many rose bushes because kangaroos kept eating all the blooms, and we were unable to find any natural deterrent against kangaroos apart from dingo urine, which isn't exactly something you can buy at the supermarket! The kangaroos show no interest at all in some of the native plants which have been used to replace the roses.

Sometimes we need to experiment with different products until we find one that works for us. Putting up protective barriers, like gauze curtains, can help fend off unwanted visitors. And it helps to keep large, empty matchboxes near points of entry in our house so that should, for example, a cockroach find his way inside, we have what we need on hand to capture and remove him (while recollecting our bodhichitta motivation). If the idea of catching a roach to release it outside revolts you, consider that in protecting its life, you are creating the cause for your own life to be protected or extended. Motivated by bodhichitta, you have empowered this protection immeasurably. What a wonderful opportunity that cockroach is presenting to you!

There may be occasions when the destruction of large numbers of beings is simply unavoidable—like the discovery of white ants in part of the wooden structure of our house. At these times, we can only do our best to minimise suffering, to recollect our bodhichitta motivation and to recite mantras and undertake the other practices previously outlined for the benefit of the many beings now entering the bardo.

Overall, given that prevention is generally so much easier than cure, the best way to deal with animal pests is to do all we can to avoid attracting them to us in the first place.

IS THERE ANYTHING I CAN DO TO DEAL WITH CONFRONTING CASES OF ANIMAL SUFFERING?

On an ongoing basis we are exposed to the reality of Buddha's First Noble Truth—the existence of suffering—especially where it concerns other sentient beings. The body of a dead animal or 'road kill' at the side of the bitumen. The pursuit of vulnerable animals by predators. Road trains filled with sheep or cattle on their way to port, and an arduous journey, followed by slaughter in a foreign abattoir. Live export ranks as one of the most oppressive forms of legalised cruelty, as well as an indictment on our society which, as Gandhi once noted, can be judged by the way its animals are treated. But what can we do as we pass another consignment of sentient beings on their way to misery and death?

Zasep Tulku Rinpoche recommends reciting the mantra of Chenrezig, the Buddha of Compassion, *Om mani padme hum*, as we send out wishes for the ultimate happiness and enlightenment of the beings on the truck. We can do the same as we pass the body of a dead animal, wishing for it to quickly achieve enlightenment. And this mantra can be used in other situations where we are bystanders but somehow wish to help. Given that animals are intuitive, and to varying extents telepathic, we should not underestimate the effect of our positive messages of support.

On a very practical basis, we can join campaigning groups as members, or at least connect with them on social media and support their activities. Whether our support is as simple as 'Liking' posts, or requires more commitment, like writing to community newspapers, lobbying local members of parliament, taking part in awareness-raising activities, or becoming ongoing financial donors, we can all contribute to the ending of inequities and cruelty. My wife and I support a number of animal charities and causes for this reason. In the case of issues like live export, in particular, I am often reminded of the well-known maxim that for evil to triumph, all it takes is for good people to do nothing.

I FEEL BAD ABOUT THE WAY I HAVE TREATED PETS OR ANIMALS IN THE PAST. IS THERE ANYTHING I CAN DO TO MAKE IT UP TO THEM?

Buddhism takes a strong line on guilt: it is a wasted emotion. Being eaten up with negativity because of the way you acted in the past is not only of no benefit to you or anyone else, it may very well hold you back from living to your full potential.

Regret, on the other hand, can be more useful. When we recognise that we have thought, said or done something we wish we hadn't, we can try to make amends. If that isn't possible, we can at the very least make a determined effort not to repeat the action.

If you are filled with regret at the memory of fishing expeditions as a teenager, catapulting birds, stamping on insects or other acts of violence and cruelty, there are things you can do. The minds of the beings you hurt still exist somewhere. In the case of pets, in particular, there is still that karmic connection. If you are a Buddhist, lamas recommend saying mantras, and dedicating your practice for the benefit of the being about whom you have regrets.

The practical steps outlined in the answer to the previous question, such as supporting animal charities, are another way to help make amends, and turn regret into a positive motivating force.

And there are other, broader-based activities you can undertake, dedicating the merit from so doing to the benefit of those you harmed. These include things like installing a birdbath in your garden and keeping it replenished with fresh water. Or a feeder, especially in winter, to sustain the birds. You can volunteer at animal shelters, or foster a pet. Participate in community clean-ups, or take it upon yourself to ensure a local pond is kept free of garbage and other waste that could be harmful to birds and other wildlife.

These are just a few suggestions to help spark your own creativity, and help transform a negative feeling about something that can't be changed, into a positive force for compassion.

I'VE HEARD OF THE BUDDHIST TRADITION OF RELEASING ANIMALS WHO HAVE BEEN CAUGHT—LIKE THE LOBSTERS YOU SEE IN AQUARIUMS AT SOME RESTAURANTS. IS THIS A USEFUL PRACTICE?

This certainly is a tradition in some Buddhist cultures, but not one that translates very well into the contemporary world. The ideas behind it are to free the animals involved, as an act of compassion, and also to cultivate the karmic causes for enjoying protection and longer life—whether in this lifetime or a future one.

There are some obvious problems when it comes to applying this practice today. If you were to head off to your nearest Chinese restaurant that has live lobsters and buy up all their stock, chances are that a fresh delivery would arrive within a very short space of time. You would therefore simply be accelerating the demand for more lobsters to be captured—the opposite of the result you seek.

Then there is the practical matter of making sure you can, in fact, release the rescued lobsters. Are you sure you can release them into an area where they can survive and flourish, and where it is legal for you to do what you are doing? And how are you going to ensure they make the journey successfully from restaurant to ocean in properly oxygenated water?

There are some markets in Asia where stallholders participate in a frenzy of bird trapping in the lead-up to Buddhist festivities, so that the locals have plenty of birds to buy up in order to release them. A grotesque aberration, surely, of the wish to practise compassion?

My own view is that the best way to bring to an end practices we find abhorrent is to vote with our wallets. To withdraw our custom from those who perpetuate cruelty and encourage others to do the same. Whether keeping lobsters in restaurant aquariums before plunging them into boiling water is any more cruel than the containment and killing practices of factory farming can be debated.

Working out the right thing to do is sometimes complex. But we may also find ourselves in situations where we can save animals from certain death without unintended consequences, and we can take joy from helping. There is the well-known tale of the man who walked along a beach, bending every so often to collect a stranded starfish to throw into the sea.

'There are miles of beach and hundreds of starfish!' observed a passer-by. 'You can't make a difference!'

Throwing a starfish into the water, the other replied, 'I made a difference to that one!'

Snails making their way across the footpath. A mouse or lizard who has been cornered by the cat. A bird that has been stunned, or is being attacked by others of its species. These all offer the opportunity to protect life and practise compassion.

Om mani padme hum!

I HAVE THE EXPERIENCE OF 'SEEING' ANIMALS AND/OR BEING AWARE OF PARTICULAR SPECIES OF ANIMALS EITHER WHILE AWAKE OR IN DREAMS. WHAT IS HAPPENING?

It is not uncommon for people to be aware of animal spirits. These may be the momentary glimpse of an appearance like our once-loved but deceased pet, or perhaps an animal with whom we have no previous connection.

I personally have had the experience of feeling like I saw the ghost of my much-loved cat entering the room. The experience lasted for a second, or even less. Do I really think it was her, manifesting in some way?

My answer is: I honestly don't know, but I doubt it. There was no purpose to the apparent sighting. No useful message was conveyed. I wasn't feeling particularly bereft of her presence at the time. Perhaps I was just imagining what happened, and a more prosaic explanation of light and wind may be the reason I thought I saw something.

This is not to say that I don't believe in ghosts. There are just too many anecdotal sightings made by too many level-headed people to dismiss the phenomena. Where I think we have to be careful is in jumping to conclusions about what the apparitions are. The truth is that we don't know enough about ghosts to be certain. Saying they are the spirits of the dead is one explanation. But what if they are the work of other, unknown entities simply taking on the appearance of the dead person for some reason, good or ill?

If the concept of rebirth is correct—and, interestingly, many psychics who say they communicate with spirits of the dead also say they believe in rebirth—there is an apparent contradiction in suggesting, on the one hand, that after death, mind finds rebirth in another form, while, on the other, claiming this same mind may manifest at various intervals, perhaps years later, taking on the appearance of its old form. Can a three-year-old boy be playing happily with his toys while simultaneously manifesting as the ghost of the much-loved dog of his former lifetime to its previous owner? Can we have it both ways?

Not understanding the workings of energy at its most subtle level, all I can say is that it is a 'known unknown'.

Our distant ancestors believed that the appearance of animal spirits, especially when they recurred—whether that of a once-loved pet, or a completely different animal—happened in order to deliver a particular message.

At the most subtle level, you may keep noticing a specific and perhaps unusual animal—say, a flamingo—incorporated into the design of items you handle, or places you visit. Perhaps this animal keeps coming up in your dreams. You don't necessarily have to 'see' a flamingo walk into your sitting room in broad daylight for the presence of flamingo-ness to penetrate your consciousness.

It doesn't really matter whether we accept the existence of animal spirits, or regard these happenings more along the lines of symbols arising from the unconscious—all arise from mind, in any case. What's interesting is the totemic significance possessed by animals, which our forebears would have understood, but which, after centuries of dislocation from nature, we have long forgotten.

If you have the experience of being especially aware of a particular animal, or identify very strongly with a particular species, I suggest you explore the world of animal totems through writers such as Ted Andrews and Scott Alexander King to help decode the symbolic significance of what you are intuitively feeling, thereby bringing to the surface a potentially life-enhancing message.

EPILOGUE

I BEGAN THIS BOOK with some of the important questions that pet lovers ask themselves—questions that, in our society, often go unanswered. Questions about how animals' minds compare to our own. What happens to their consciousness when they die. How interactions with them may be significant in ways that go way beyond the immediate here and now.

I very much hope the insights offered, from the perspective of Tibetan Buddhism, help in your own personal search for answers.

In writing this book, I also hope to be contributing to a broader social awakening. We are living in an era of unprecedented discovery, exploring the intelligent life that may exist not only on distant planets in our universe but, more importantly, right under our own noses. Scarcely a week goes by without the results of some new research program or case study showing that animals use their own language, or act with empathy and compassion, or possess sensory—and sometimes extra-sensory—perceptions that humans can't possibly match.

The collective impact of these revelations challenges long-held assumptions about *Homo sapien's* place on planet earth. Step by step, they are also bringing scientific consensus to the position long held by Buddhists: that animals are thinking, feeling, conscious beings.

The ethical implications of this radical reframing are explained with great lucidity and power in the works of authors such as Matthieu

Ricard and Peter Singer. It is the very personal implications, for the way we relate to our pets, that concerns us here. How might we summarise these implications for the inner life of pets?

PETS HAVE THE SAME CAPACITY FOR SPIRITUALITY THAT WE DO

The starting point is that beneath our obvious physical and mental differences, we and our pets share the same essential nature and the same consciousness. We all wish for happiness and to avoid suffering, and the means by which we achieve these things are often remarkably similar. We may not share a developed language, although our pets generally pay far closer attention to our communication than we do to theirs. But far from being mere playthings—inferior, morally irrelevant and ultimately dispensable—a growing body of research studies is confirming what many animal lovers already take for granted, which is that qualities once regarded as uniquely human are shared by many sentient beings. In particular, animals demonstrate the same capacity for those behaviours traditionally seen as the hallmark of a spiritual life—empathy, compassion, fairness and altruism.

SIMPLE PRESENCE IS THE START OF A DEEPER CONNECTION

As pet lovers we may spend a lot of time talking to our animal companions, but how much time do we spend listening to them?

As a society, long dislocated from nature, human minds have become dysfunctionally busy, a trend that has dramatically increased with the proliferation of mobile devices and online media. The much quieter minds of other animals, far from indicating diminished capacity, may suggest that they are not only more attuned to their own consciousness, but to ours too. Many pets appear able to access a more subtle mental bandwidth, better enabling them to demonstrate abilities like telepathy, which humans experience much more rarely. Offering the optimal environment for our pets, and making a regular point of being mindfully present for them, can profoundly shift the dynamics of the way that we and our pets relate.

MEDITATION CAN HAVE POWERFUL BENEFITS

Along with being more mindfully present for our pets, regular meditation offers powerful benefits on many levels. A common response of meditators is that they become like magnets to their pets when they sit on the cushion. Pets intuitively respond to our efforts to calm our own minds. They are attracted by our shift in consciousness, and feel reassured and more trusting. Difficult relationships between pets and humans can be resolved by the gentle but profound impact of meditation, and close relationships can become even deeper. Meditation helps pets through times of transition, such as house moves and family changes.

Meditation also offers healing, the word 'meditation' deriving from the same source as 'medication', meaning to make whole. Just as self-repair in humans has been shown in clinical studies to be boosted by meditation, we can help our pets self-repair by meditating with them, perhaps because they appear to have the capacity to entrain their minds with our own. There is anecdotal evidence that pain management, the speed of recovery from surgery, and the impact of side-effects can all benefit by meditating with our pets when they are ill.

PETS ARE NOT IN OUR LIVES BY ACCIDENT: THEIR PRESENCE IS AN EXTRAORDINARY PRIVILEGE

Most of us accept that our world view is shaped by the ongoing interplay of cause and effect, beginning with formative experiences in our childhood. Buddhism suggests that these same dynamics actually play out over lifetimes. This view has many startling implications for pet lovers.

Are the beings with whom we share our homes here by accident? Beneath conventional explanations of, say, a trip to the animal shelter, could the dynamics of causality offer an underlying reason? If the pets with whom we share our lives have been very significant to us before, we now have the opportunity to repay past kindnesses, as well as offer them the best possible preparation for their futures. There are many ways we can help achieve this, through practices like mantra recitation and meditation, avoiding exposure to violence and aggression, and recollecting bodhichitta throughout each day.

If you are not quite ready to believe that causality, or karma, stretches over lifetimes—that's fine. These are the very same practices most likely to cultivate wellbeing in *this* lifetime, for our pets, as well as ourselves.

WE CAN BE OF IMMENSE BENEFIT AT THE TIME OF ILLNESS AND DEATH

Pet lovers typically experience the impending death of their animal companions as a very traumatic period, accompanied by feelings of helplessness and loss. Buddhism offers a radically different perspective on this time of transition. When we place our pets' needs, rather than our own feelings, at the centre of what is happening, and engage in practices designed to help our animals when they can most benefit from our support, we have the opportunity to transform our experience of what is happening.

Drawing on the love and devotion we feel for our pet to be of extraordinary service to them, both during the death process and for seven weeks afterwards, we can act with purpose and compassion to benefit our pet through a time of vital transition.

REBIRTH OPENS UP PANORAMIC POSSIBILITIES

Do our beloved companions return to us? Would we recognise them if they did? And what of the beings in our lives with whom we are already intimately connected? The concept of rebirth has fascinating implications, and there are compelling accounts of both human and animal rebirths which illuminate exactly such possibilities.

Given that most of us are not clairvoyant, we can only guess at the shared relationships that exist. Of more immediate relevance is the understanding that we possess an opportunity to be a force for good in this lifetime. To heal past wounds. To make the most positive impact on the lives of those closest to us. With this more panoramic perspective, part of our life's mission is to do all we can to ensure that, as and when we meet up again in the future with those who have played an important part in our lives, it will be in the most benevolent and auspicious way.

OTHER ANIMALS ARE NO DIFFERENT FROM OUR PETS

While most of our focus has been on our relationship with pets, there are clear implications for the spiritual lives of all creatures, great and small. How authentic is our wish to cultivate compassion on the one hand if, on the other, we support the systematic exploitation of animals through factory farming? Confronted by the myriad horrors inflicted on animals, especially by our fellow humans, is there anything we can do to cope with feelings of being overwhelmed and helpless? And what if we are haunted by our own past behaviour towards animals, which may have been less than enlightened?

Buddhism offers both practical suggestions as well as psychological tools to help us towards greater coherence. Whether we, as individuals, tend more towards activism or contemplation, there is much we can do to play our part in the gathering momentum towards the global recognition that human wellbeing is inextricably linked to the wellbeing of other species.

GIFTS AND BENEFICIARIES

As pet lovers, we value the unaffected love and connection we share with our companions. That purr in the middle of the night, and the reach of a velvet paw as our cat acknowledges that we have surfaced—perhaps momentarily—from deep sleep. The tail-wagging frenzy as we step through the front door and are reminded that there is more to life than whatever has been burdening us all the way home. The swoop of our parrot from a perch, onto our shoulder, welcoming us back into his presence. With our pets, unlike the vast majority of sentient beings, we can be unaffectedly ourselves. Their simple acceptance, along with the way that they draw us constantly into the present, are among their most constant and frequent gifts.

But they offer far greater gifts than these.

I never cease to be astonished by how much attention, intense scrutiny and passionate debate our society focuses on things like politics, property prices and interest rates—subjects of great importance, to be sure, but which are relevant to us for only as long as we are alive. If there is something about us that endures, surely *that* opens the door to even more important questions? Questions like: what is it, exactly, that may continue? Is there a relationship between my experience of reality now and how I may experience reality after death? If so, how can I ensure the most positive outcome, both for myself and others? And what of those relationships with others: does conventional reality provide a full account of how they have come into my life, or could a deeper set of dynamics be at play?

Day-to-day life very rarely invites us to explore these *really* important questions. But our pets do. Facing the terminal illness of our beloved companion, what pet lover doesn't worry about what will happen to this being who has been so utterly dependent on us? Or question if some part of them may continue? Or simply wonder what is the best way to help them face their own death?

In prompting these questions, our pets may do more for us than even some of our dearest friends. For in asking questions about their spiritual lives, we come to face our own. That dimension of our existence that we may routinely ignore, or postpone till some mythical point in the future when we have more time, can no longer be avoided: we are spiritual beings too.

If it is our pets who bring us to this recognition, if it is they who encourage us to cultivate love and compassion, and to act in accord with our highest nature, then what are they doing if not carrying out the work of enlightened beings? Who is the ultimate beneficiary in this relationship?!

We sometimes hear it said, when people bring home a dog or cat from a rescue centre, that although they saved the pet by giving it a home, in reality the pet saved them. And this may be what they mean. The spiritual lives of pets are inextricably bound up with our own spiritual lives. As outlined in this book, there is much we can do to contribute to the wellbeing and development of our closest companions. The counterpoint is that in giving us the opportunity to be our kindest and most virtuous selves, our pets offer us gifts of inestimable value.

As we chart our journey towards an understanding of our own ultimate nature, our greatest mutual supporters in our search for abiding happiness may be found on our lap, perched on our shoulder, or sitting on the front doormat, leash in mouth, with an expression of irresistible expectation.

GLOSSARY

bardo A transitional or intermediate state between death and rebirth

bodhichitta Literally 'the mind of enlightenment'. The aspiration to achieve enlightenment to free all living beings from suffering

bodhisattva A person who wishes to attain enlightenment to free all living beings from suffering

Buddha Literally 'awakened one'; a fully awakened being who has attained enlightenment

Dependent Arising The concept that every person and object only exists by depending on other factors

Dharma The doctrine or teachings of the Buddha

enlightenment A state in which the mind is awakened to its true nature, which is boundless, omniscient, compassionate, blissful and ultimately beyond conception

guru Spiritual friend

karma Literally 'action' or 'deed'. Implies 'reaction', and the concept of cause and effect

mantra Literally 'mind protection'. In practice, a collection of sounds recited in connection with a particular meditation to achieve a particular outcome

nirvana Literally 'to extinguish' the false sense of self. Generally refers to personal liberation from samsara

samsara   Mind afflicted by karma and delusion. It is this mind that perpetuates the universal cycle of birth, death and rebirth by grasping at the false sense of self

Sangha   The community of Buddhist monks and nuns. In the West the term 'lay sangha' refers to practitioners who have not been ordained

tantra   The advanced teachings of Tibetan Buddhism practised only after initiations

Tulku   A recognised reincarnate lama. One who has voluntarily been reborn to help others to enlightenment

ENDNOTES

INTRODUCTION

1 Francis Crick, *The Astonishing Hypothesis: The scientific search for the soul,* Scribner, New York, 1994, p. 3.
2 See: http://escholarship.org/uc/item/8sx4s79c#page-8, accessed 10 February 2016.
3 Carl Safina, *Beyond Words: What animals think and feel,* Henry Holt & Company LLC, New York, 2015, p. 69.
4 Linda Bender, *Animal Wisdom: Learning from the spiritual lives of animals,* North Atlantic Books, Berkeley, CA, 2014, pp. 28–9.
5 Rupert Sheldrake, *The Sense of Being Stared At: And other aspects of the extended mind,* Arrow Books, London, 2004, p. 85.

CHAPTER ONE

1 Carl Safina, *Beyond Words: What animals think and feel,* Henry Holt & Company LLC, New York, 2015, p. 169.
2 See: http://www.dailymail.co.uk/news/article-3501272/Your-dog-read-mind-knows-think-people.html, accessed 21 March 2016.
3 See: https://www.psychologytoday.com/blog/canine-corner/201206/canine-empathy-your-dog-really-does-care-if-you-are-unhappy, accessed 21 March 2016.
4 See: http://www.thetimes.co.uk/article/dog-breaks-window-to-get-help-for-ill-owner-rpfv60v2n, accessed 4 October 2016.
5 See: abcnews.go.com/US/rescued-dog-saves-sleeping-family-fire/story?id=26021233, accessed 23 November 2016.
6 Rupert Sheldrake, *The Sense of Being Stared At: And other aspects of the extended mind,* Arrow Books, London, 2004, p. 83.
7 See: https://en.wikipedia.org/wiki/Bubastis, accessed 14 March 2016.

8 See: www.medicalnewstoday.com/articles/98432.php, accessed 14 March 2017.
9 John Bradshaw, *Cat Sense: How the new feline science can make you a better friend*, Penguin Books, London, 2013, p. 64.
10 See: http://www.npr.org/sections/13.7/2015/01/22/379008858/mind-your-moods-cat-owners, accessed 22 March 2016.
11 John Bradshaw, *Cat Sense*, p. 234.
12 See: http://pubpages.unh.edu/~jel/Descartes.html, accessed 16 March 2016.
13 Carl Safina, *Beyond Words*, p. 81.

CHAPTER TWO

1 See: http://www.scientificamerican.com/article/what-are-dogs-saying-when-they-bark/, accessed 23 March 2016. Brian Hare and Vanessa Woods, *The Genius of Dogs: How dogs are smarter than you think*, Dutton Adult, New York, 2013.
2 Carl Safina, *Beyond Words: What animals think and feel*, Henry Holt & Company LLC, New York, 2015, p. 67.
3 Carl Safina, *Beyond Words*, p. 93.
4 Carl Safina, *Beyond Words*, p. 291.
5 See: http://www.nytimes.com/2007/09/11/science/11parrot.html?_r=0, accessed 16 March 2016.
6 Irene M. Pepperberg, *Alex & Me: How a scientist and a parrot discovered a hidden world of animal intelligence—and formed a deep bond in the process*, Scribe Publications Pty Ltd, Melbourne, 2009, p. 214.
7 Rupert Sheldrake, *Dogs That Know When Their Owners Are Coming Home*, Broadway Books, New York, 2011.
8 You can watch a video showing excerpts of this experiment at: www.mind-energy.net/archives/628-A-short-video-of-the-psychic-parrot-NKisi.html
9 See: http://pulptastic.com/lulu-the-pig/, accessed 23 November 2016.
10 Frans de Waal, *The Bonobo and The Atheist: In search of humanism among the primates*, W.W. Norton & Company Ltd, New York, 2015, p. 17.
11 See: chicago.cbslocal.com/2011/08/16/15-years-ago-today-gorilla-rescues-boy-who-fell-in-ape-pit/
12 See: https://www.facebook.com/raju.sa.790/videos/582184275216295/, accessed 18 March 2016.
13 See: http://www.livescience.com/17378-rats-show-empathy.html, accessed 18 March 2016.
14 See: http://www.telegraph.co.uk/news/2016/06/07/fish-can-recognise-human-faces/, accessed 9 June 2016.
15 See: https://www.psychologytoday.com/blog/animal-emotions/201406/fish-are-sentient-and-emotional-beings-and-clearly-feel-pain, accessed 9 June 2016.

16 Victoria Braithwaite, *Do Fish Feel Pain?*, Oxford University Press, Oxford, 2010, p. 153.

17 Albert Einstein, *The Expanded Quotable Einstein*, Alice Calaprice (ed.), Princeton University Press, Princeton, NJ, 2000, p. 316.

18 His Holiness Dalai Lama XIV, *The Dalai Lama: A policy of kindness*, Snow Lion Publications, Ithaca, New York, 1990, p. 112.

19 The Cambridge Declaration on Consciousness was written by Philip Low and edited by Jaak Panksepp, Diana Reiss, David Edelman, Bruno Van Swinderen, Philip Low and Christof Koch.

20 Laurens van der Post, *The Lost World of the Kalahari*, Vintage, London, 2002, p. 236.

21 See: A.P. Elkin, *Aboriginal Men of High Degree: Initiation and sorcery in the world's oldest tradition*, Inner Traditions, Vermont, 1993.

CHAPTER FOUR

1 See: http://news.harvard.edu/gazette/story/2010/11/wandering-mind-not-a-happy-mind/, accessed 20 March 2016.

2 Translated and reproduced with kind permission of Keith Dowman, verse from *Tilopa's Mahamudra Instruction to Naropa in Twenty-eight Verses*.

3 Julian F. Pas, *The Wisdom of the Tao*, Oneworld Publications, Oxford, 2000, p. 206, attributed to Liezi 2: 'The Yellow Emperor', translated by A.C. Graham, p. 55.

CHAPTER FIVE

1 See: http://www.takepart.com/article/2013/05/16/can-dolphins-detect-cancer-in-humans, accessed 5 April 2016.

2 See: https://www.dogsforgood.org/how-we-help/assistance-dog/autism-assistance-dogs-children/, accessed 30 December 2016.

CHAPTER SIX

1 See: http://www.dogmeditation.com/purchaseinfo.html, accessed 7 April 2015.

CHAPTER SEVEN

1 Geshe Acharya Thubten Loden, *Path to Enlightenment in Tibetan Buddhism*, Tushita Publications, Melbourne, 1993, p. 367.

2 Geshe Acharya Thubten Loden, *Path to Enlightenment in Tibetan Buddhism*, p. 367.

3 E.H. Johnston, *Asvaghosa's Buddhacarita or Acts of the Buddha*. Complete Sanskrit text with English translation. Motilal Banarsidass Publishers Limited, Delhi, India, 1995 reprint.

4 His Holiness Dalai Lama XIV, *A Flash of Lightning in the Dark of Night*, Shambhala Publications Inc., Boston, MA, 1994, p. 18.

5 From Acharya Zasep Tulku Rinpoche, *Tara in the Palm of Your Hand: A guide to the practice of the twenty-one Taras*, Wind Horse Press, Nelson, 2013, p. 11.

CHAPTER EIGHT

1 B.H. Lipton, *The Biology of Belief: Unleashing the power of consciousness, matter and miracles*, Hay House, Carslbad, CA, 2008, p. 32.

2 Thorwald Dethlefsen and Ruediger Dahlke, *The Healing Power of Illness: The meaning of symptoms and how to interpret them*, Element Books Ltd, Dorset, 1990, p. 13.

3 David Michie, *Why Mindfulness Is Better Than Chocolate: Your guide to inner peace, enhanced focus and deep happiness*, Allen & Unwin, Sydney, 2014, pp. 265–8.

4 See: http://www.cancerresearchuk.org/about-cancer/cancers-in-general/treatment/complementary-alternative/therapies/meditation, accessed 13 June 2016.

CHAPTER NINE

1 Professor Richard Gregory, 'Brainy Mind', www.richardgregory.org/papers/brainy_mind/brainy-mind.htm, accessed 7 May 2016 (originally published in the *British Medical Journal*, 1998, vol. 317, pp. 1693–5).

2 Thomas J. McFarlane (ed.), *Einstein and Buddha: The parallel sayings*, Ulysses Press, Berkeley, CA, 2002, p. 64.

3 See: www.iaahpc.org/about/what-is-animal-hospice.html/

4 Tulku Thondup, *Peaceful Death, Joyful Rebirth: A Tibetan Buddhist guidebook*, Shambhala Publications Inc., Boston, MA, 2006, p. 20.

5 Tulku Thondup, *Peaceful Death, Joyful Rebirth*, p. 20.

CHAPTER TEN

1 Geshe Acharya Thubten Loden, *Path to Enlightenment in Tibetan Buddhism*, Tushita Publications, Melbourne, 1993, p. 401.

2 See:http://www.dimattinacoffee.com.au/blog/entry/gino_reincarnated,accessed 4 October 2016.

3 See video interview embedded in article at: http://reluctant-messenger.com/reincarnation-proof.htm, accessed 18 May 2016.

FURTHER READING

Ted Andrews, *Animal-Wise: Understanding the language of animal messengers and companions*, Dragonhawk Publishing, Jackson, TN, 2009.

John Bradshaw, *Cat Sense: How the new feline science can make you a better friend*, Penguin Books, London, 2013.

Thorwald Dethlefsen and Ruediger Dahkle, *The Healing Power of Illness: The meaning of symptoms and how to interpret them*, Element Books Ltd, Dorset, 1990.

Frans de Waal, *The Bonobo and The Atheist: In search of humanism among the primates*, W.W. Norton & Company Ltd, New York, 2015.

Andy Fraser (ed.), *The Healing Power of Meditation: Leading experts on buddhism, psychology, and medicine explore the health benefits of contemplative practice*, Shambhala Publications Inc., Boston, MA, 2013.

Scott Alexander King, *Animal Messenger: Interpreting the symbolic language of the world's animals*, New Holland, Sydney, 2006.

David Michie, *Buddhism for Busy People: Finding happiness in an uncertain world*, Allen & Unwin, Sydney, 2004.

David Michie, *Enlightenment To Go: The classic Buddhist path of compassion and transformation*, Allen & Unwin, Sydney, 2010.

David Michie, *Why Mindfulness Is Better Than Chocolate: Your guide to inner peace, enhanced focus and deep happiness*, Allen & Unwin, Sydney, 2014.

Irene M. Pepperberg, *Alex & Me: How a scientist and a parrot discovered a hidden world of animal intelligence—and formed a deep bond in the process*, Scribe Publications Pty Ltd, Melbourne, 2009.

Kathleen Prasad, *How to Help Animals with Reiki*, Amazon Digital Services, 2015.

Matthieu Riccard, *A Plea for the Animals: The moral, philosophical and evolutionary imperative to treat all beings with compassion*, Shambhala Publications Inc., Boston, MA, 2016.

Carl Safina, *Beyond Words: What animals think and feel*, Henry Holt & Company LLC, New York, 2015.

Rupert Sheldrake, *Dogs That Know When Their Owners Are Coming Home*, Broadway Books, New York, 2011.

Rupert Sheldrake, *The Sense of Being Stared At: And other unexplained powers of human minds*, Park Street Press, New York, 2013.

Jennifer Skiff, *The Divinity of Dogs: True stories of miracles inspired by man's best friend*, Allen & Unwin, Sydney, 2013.

Tulku Thondup, *Peaceful Death, Joyful Rebirth: A Tibetan Buddhist guidebook*, Shambhala Publications Inc., Boston, MA, 2006.

Geshe Acharya Thubten Loden, *Path to Enlightenment in Tibetan Buddhism*, Tushita Publications, Melbourne, 1993.

Acharya Zasep Tulku Rinpoche, *Tara in the Palm of Your Hand: A guide to the practice of the twenty-one Taras*, Wind Horse Press, Nelson, 2013.

Acharya Zasep Tulku Rinpoche, *A Tulku's Journey from Tibet to Canada*, Wind Horse Press, Nelson, 2016.

ACKNOWLEDGEMENTS

MY GRATEFUL THANKS, FIRST and foremost, to all those readers who have bought this and my previous books. It is only your support that enables me to keep writing.

I also sincerely appreciate all the wisdom and support of Gail Pope, founder of BrightHaven; Kathleen Prasad, founder of Animal Reiki Source; Carolyn Trethewey, founder of Pause HQ; and Mel Keen, founder of Horse Horizons, each of whose practical experience of mindful encounters with animals is a continuing source of inspiration to many people around the world.

I feel so fortunate to have been contacted by readers with many fascinating stories involving their pets. In particular, my very great thanks to those whose accounts I have shared in this book: Rhea Baldino, Noelene Bolton, Marjolijne de Groot, Rebecca Hartman, Jane Johnson, Salin Joseph, Belinda Joubert, Helen Rose, Judy Sampson-Hobson and Allen Wilson. There were also many other readers who wrote to me, in some cases at great length. I wish I could have shared each one of your often intriguing experiences. Alas, space constraints made this impossible.

Keith Dowman kindly gave me permission to quote his translation of the extraordinarily lucid and beautiful verses by Tilopa on the nature of mind, and I gratefully acknowledge Stephen Batchelor for his wonderful translation of Shantideva's verses.

During my life I have enjoyed the close companionship of many pets, who I would like to remember here. Their unquestioning acceptance and warm friendship inform my own experience of animal consciousness, and make me all the more passionate about encouraging my fellow humans to shift their perceptions of the many, non-human beings with whom we share our lives.

I have a habit of nicknaming friends and family members. The highest acclaim is to be named after an animal. My darling wife Koala—we met while living in London, I was from Africa and she was from Australia—has always been unreservedly supportive of my writing activities. Once again, this book owes much to her loving encouragement.

I owe the profoundest debt of gratitude to Les Sheehy, Director of the Tibetan Buddhist Society in Perth, who has taught me most of what I know about the Dharma, and who is an embodiment of compassionate wisdom in action. Without the peerless Geshe Acharya Thubten Loden, founder of the Tibetan Buddhist Society, whose books form the basis of our teaching program, I would never have had the confidence to embark on writing about the Dharma.

When this project was still in its early stages, I received warm encouragement from the Venerable Acharya Zasep Tulku Rinpoche, guru, yogi and extraordinary being. Words cannot express my heartfelt appreciation for his support, and for the generous endorsement he has offered this book.

Printed in Great Britain
by Amazon

30826272R00139